VALERIE B___ BIOGRAPHY

MW00914903

BEYOND THE CAMERA

Jason Michael Blaede

BEYOND THE CAMERA

VALERIE BERTINELLI

Biography

CONTENTS

INTRODUCTION

Valerie Bertinelli, a beloved actress, Food Network personality, and New York Times bestselling book, comments on life at sixty and beyond. Valerie Bertinli's life has not been easy behind the pleasant on-screen demeanour, especially when it comes to her own self-image and self-worth. For years, she waged a war on herself, learning to associate her worth with her image as a child star on One Day at a Time and punished herself in order to fit into the unattainable Hollywood mould. Despite the rifts produced by the rock-star lifestyle, she strove to make her marriage to Eddie Van Halen—the true love of her life—work. She then saw her son follow in his father's footsteps, all the way up to the stage of Van Halen concerts, and launch his own music career. And, like so many other women, she cared for her parents as their health deteriorated, reversing the roles of parent and child. Valerie eventually shouted, "Enough already!" to a lifelong fight with the scale and found a new road forward to joy and connection after mourning the death of her parents, learning more about her family's background, and recognizing how brief life truly is when she and her son lost Eddie. Despite adversity and the media industry's pushes to be someone she isn't, Valerie is now accepting herself: she understands who she is, has established her self-worth, and has learnt how to prioritise her health and happiness over her weight. Enough Already is the narrative of Valerie's sometimes amusing, sometimes emotional, but always honest journey to love yourself and find joy in the daily, in family, and in the food and memories we share, with an intimate glimpse into her fears, heartbreaks, losses, successes, and insights.

"This thoughtful, bighearted book is sure to please Bertinelli fans and those looking for stories about hard-won self-acceptance." "A warmly personal memoir."

CHAPTER 1

THE CLOCK IS TICKING

OCTOBER 2019

Wolfie has been working on his first album, which does not yet have a release date, but he does have more than a dozen songs that I want him to put on my phone so I can listen to them anytime I want, which will be basically all the time. Yes, I am a proud mother—and with reason. He wrote all of the tunes and played all of the instruments. I think the tunes are fantastic. I'm hoping the dip will buy me enough time to listen, get him to help me with the download, and ask all kinds of mom questions. When he has had enough of my interrogation, I will say, "How about that dip?"

The strategy is effective. When I visit Wolfie, I go right to the kitchen, like I usually do. I frequently bring groceries or a meal to reheat. It's the cheesy spinach and crab dip this time. He has a sleek, modern kitchen that leads to a living and dining room. It has the feel of a light and airy loft. I preheat the oven and prepare the dip. I wash my hands on a dish towel that I vaguely recall purchasing for him a while back and ask Wolfie what's new. He updates me on several topics before casually saying, "By the way, Dad is on his way over."

"Dad" is my ex-husband and buddy Edward Van Halen, also known as Ed to me.

"That's great," I say. "I haven't seen him in a long time." "How is he doing?"

"He's okay," Wolfie says.

Wolfie tells me that Ed called when I was on my way to his place. He was out running errands with his assistant when he asked if he may pay us a visit. Ed knocks and opens the door a few minutes later, as I am laying the warm dip on the kitchen counter. He comes to a halt a few feet inside after hearing Wolfie's music on the sound system. His face breaks into a wide grin. "How about this kid?" he asks as we embrace. "I know," I admit. "My heart is melting."

Ed and I separated in 2007 after we stopped living together in 2002. We both remarried, but in our own ways, we remained together. We've spent four decades together, sharing love, anger, frustration, friendship, and love. Love is what has endured. That is the lesson I have learnt, and continue to learn, particularly these days.

The same is true for Ed, who was diagnosed with tongue cancer in 2000 and has since battled several types of the disease. He's been having a particularly difficult time recently. That is what makes seeing him eat with such relish such a pleasant occasion. He is still devilishly cute at 64 years old. But, for the time being, what counts most is that he still seems to enjoy my cooking. We are all mortal. Our lives have three parts: beginning, middle, and end. It seems to happen without much thought outside of life's most important and inescapable moments: graduations, marriages, breakups, birthdays, and deaths. Most of us see life as a gradual ascent up a ladder. It's punctuated by various anniversaries, such as turning forty, fifty, sixty, and so on. Our children grow up, leave the nest, and start their own lives. We become empty nesters and have to rethink our lifestyles. We find ourselves caring for our parents and, eventually, saying our final goodbyes to them.

I had firsthand knowledge of this. All of the above had happened to me. But the ladder we're ascending will inevitably wobble. Nothing awful happens, but it moves again later, this time a little harder—or maybe a lot harder, hard enough to knock you off your feet. Ed's wobble occurred when he was initially diagnosed with cancer. It got to the point where he was holding on so he wouldn't fall off.

At that point, he realised that the most valuable asset he possessed, and the only thing that mattered, was time. Wolfie, who was just in his mid-twenties, was also aware of this. I have an uncanny ability to not think about such things until I have no choice, at which point I can't. It's why Wolfie and Ed withhold some information regarding Ed's condition from me. They don't want me to be concerned any more than I already am. So, while I don't know the depth of Ed's condition, I know it's serious, and given how quickly he devours my spinach and crab dip, I want to do something kind for him.

"You should come over here and I'll make you bami," I suggest.

Wendie Malick once said to me while I was working on Hot in Cleveland, "Before we met, I had this impression of you as a sweet, timid little thing." But you're a really good truck driver." It's impossible for me to deny. I'm like a bull in a china shop. I am also a fanatical New Orleans Saints fan, and the Saints are playing in one of three NFL games on Thanksgiving Day, so I am among those who come in and out of the room to check on the action.

On one of these trips, I happen to see Ed as he goes in the front door. I give him a hug and a kiss, noting that he looks exactly the same as he did a few weeks before, if not better. I notice a gleam in his eyes that indicates his joy at being with us at the house. I'm delighted he came, that he's feeling well enough to engage in the rituals of being together as a family—acknowledging our links, re-establishing our bonds to each other, discussing, reminiscing, laughing, and eating as much as we can hold. As I encourage Ed to relax and remind him that I have made bami for him, he is already smiling and nodding at others. He takes a long breath, savouring the many odours drifting from the kitchen, and exclaims, "It smells delicious."

"I certainly hope so," I say.

I spent a few days in December with Wolfie and Andraia in our old residence in Park City, Utah. Wolfie and I had been planning this vacation for years. When Wolfie was a preschooler, Ed and I bought this ancient 1890s mining shack and sold it approximately ten years later. We always felt bad about doing this. Wolfie discovered the place on Airbnb in early 2019, which he instantly showed me, and stated, "I really want all of us to go there again." You, me, Dad, and all of our pals. People can come and go. It'll be like old times."

I adored the concept. We all did. As a result, I did something I seldom do: I planned ahead and reserved the house for Christmas and New Year's.

Wolfie tries to cancel his flight to Park City. Ed needs surgery, and Wolfie wants to be there for him. I inform him that Ed's carer will be with him, that Park City is only an hour's flight from Los Angeles if he has to return, and that I am concerned about him as his mother. I can tell he needs some time apart to unwind.

I am also correct. As soon as we enter the house, I observe Wolfie's shoulders relax and hear him breathe more easily. He laughs and jokes even more. He mocks my delight at coming back here. I can't help myself—and don't want to. I can sense our past in the air. Even though the house appears to have been remodelled several times since our last visit, it's as if we hung our memories in the closet when we left, and they are still there.

When we lived here, the little house featured an open floor design and a notable quirk: the floor sloped. The entire home was slanted. Wolfie was able to push one of his Matchbox cars from his bedroom and see it roll all the way to the front door. I overheard him telling Andraia about it, as well as other things from our stay here. He was a tiny boy back then, and he was only thirteen when we sold the house, but I can hear him recalling so many events with such colour and humour that I couldn't help but smile. We apparently accomplished a couple things correctly as parents.

He and Andraia wish to go for a walk into town. I follow them outside and stand on the front porch, watching them walk down the street. I enjoy taking in the fresh alpine air. This property has always had a cheerful feel, which I am thrilled to see is still present. Later that night, we FaceTimed Ed and told him how much we missed him.

"Me, too," he says. "Perhaps we can all go back once this is over and I'm feeling better."

"Definitely," I say.

"Love you, Pop," Wolfie says.

It's strange how we've come here to reestablish a sense of family, and despite Ed's absence, we manage to pull it off. He's with us in spirit and via FaceTime. I'm only here for a few days; Wolfie and Andraia are staying till New Year's. Except for a few walks, I don't feel like going out. Cooking for them is my method of unwinding and spending quality time with them. I cook turkey meatball soup and chicken Marbella. Tonight's dish is shrimp scampi with zoodles, which is India's favourite.

The careful, systematic preparation relaxes me; it's almost like meditating. The perfume of garlic and butter fills the home while the ingredients simmer. This is the aroma of love meeting divinity. It's all the proof I need to know that God not only exists, but also wears an apron and, in my case, is most likely Italian.

The light begins to fade, and it will soon go behind the mountains. The air is crisp and clean. I'm one of those people that ends up checking up old addresses on Google while I'm seeking for something in my life, and here I am. Park City has always had a particular place in my heart. I missed the house and the love I put into it. I missed how I felt in that house, yet returning gives me a taste of it all over again.

Wolfie and Andraia return from their walk. I hear them laughing before they enter. Their cheeks are flushed from the cold. That's a picture worth remembering, I tell myself. I am a contented mother. Wolfie informs me that the walk was fantastic and that dinner smelled fantastic. Then he takes out his phone and holds it up for me to see. He claims to have received a text from his father.

"What exactly did he say?" I ask.

"He said, 'You're awesome, and I love you.'"

CHAPTER 2

ENOUGH ALREADY

DECEMBER 2019

The new year is weighing heavily on me. In early January, I'll be doing a food segment on the Today show. The show offered me the opportunity to become a more permanent member of the Today family without having to relocate to New York. I thought it was a great concept. I feel smarter and more knowledgeable when I'm around Hoda Kotb, Savannah Guthrie, Al Roker, Natalie Morales, Carson Daly, and the rest of the on-air talent and their producers.

In my first session, I'll demonstrate how to create a simple, healthy lunch and discuss my top New Year's resolution: losing ten pounds. The production team conducted research and discovered that reducing weight and eating healthy are two of the most common resolutions people make each year. I am one of those individuals. Every year, I make a resolution to lose ten pounds, exercise more, eat healthier, and so on. This is probably one of the reasons they want me on the show. My flaws are more than merely relatable. They are popular.

"It can't just be about weight anymore," I say.

I'm on the phone with the producer of the Today show.

"I've been losing the same ten pounds for the past fifty years." It's not 10 pounds. I'm sick of hearing about it. I've had it my entire life, and I'm not sure if it's really important. What I'm curious about is how I can appreciate myself as I am right now. Within this body. At my age."

I may never be able to lose the weight. I'd lose it and keep it off if I could. But... and this is a big but (pun intended)... Since I was thirteen, I've spent practically every day getting on the scale in the morning and afternoon, and I've never been happy or content with the results. That's over 32,000 steps on and off the scale, all of which ended in disappointment. My journal is a chronicle of disappointment and failure. I've been weighing myself every day without ever seeing the correct figure. Why have I conditioned my pleasure on a number that can never satisfy me?

Enough is enough.

This is a new direction for me, with a new message for everyone who has followed me on my journey. I meant what I said previously, but I think I'm finally getting to the bottom of it. I've spent most of my life, like so many others, believing that I need to lose weight and fix myself. Life has been a constant cycle of denial, criticism, and punishment. I've been pursuing a supposedly healthy appearance at the expense of my mental health. I no longer want to treat myself in this manner. I don't want to talk to myself in that manner any longer.

I'm finished evaluating myself. I don't want to consider myself overweight or slim. I don't want to weigh myself every day. It's not working, and it's clear that it's not allowing me to look in the mirror and see the greatest version of myself at the time.

If I am to assess myself, I want it to be for the right reasons: am I a giving, compassionate human being who appreciates the gift of life, beginning with my own?

"Enough already," I say to my Today show producer. "I'll be sixty years old soon." "I need to get my act together."

This suggestion is well received. The production wheels turn. Natalie Morales plans to interview me at home. I scheduled a flight to New York and got ready for an in-studio interview with Hoda and the crew. Everyone is ecstatic about this move to something far more profound and illuminating than another diet narrative. When I get off the phone, I wonder what I did. I am the type of person who hides behind a smile, a joke, a glib "Everything's fine," or a chirpy "It's all good"—even when it isn't, as has been the case recently. My father died in 2016, and my mother died this past June, despite my best efforts to care for her. I ate myself through the sadness and stress as a means of coping. And now I'm scared for Ed, as well as Wolfie. What am I doing? By attempting to improve my sausage and peppers dish.

CHAPTER 3

THE WORLD'S BEST EGGS

MARCH 2020

Love.

Ed and I had always planned to start a family. We put off trying again after I miscarried a few years into our marriage in order to focus on our professions. But by 1990, I was ready. We were building our dream house in Coldwater Canyon after ten years of marriage, with enough space for three or four children. My TV show, Sydney, had recently been cancelled when I was thirty years old. Nothing was on my mind. "Let's really try now," I told Ed, and two and a half weeks later I found out I was pregnant.

I was never happier than when this new life was growing inside of me. At first, I felt like Wonder Woman. Then, about six weeks into my pregnancy, I developed severe morning nausea that continued throughout the day and night. I sucked on lemons to get rid of the nausea, but I reminded myself that the illness and other changes in my body were all part of this incredible experience, and that I should learn to embrace it.

I also realised that eating relieved my nausea. As a result, I ate. But I didn't let up on the pressure I put on myself to get parenting just right (whatever that meant). In addition to reading all of the literature, I frequently questioned my mother. I felt as if I needed to know everything there was to know about delivery and childrearing. I was filled with dread. I wanted to get everything just right. I was determined not to make any mistakes. Finally, my mother advised me to unwind.

Angie Johnsey gave me essentially the same advice thirty years later. Just in a different setting.

Relax.

Believe your intuition.

Everything will be alright.

Motherhood is a marathon. Play it like that. This is only the beginning.

Later that night, Ed drove me to Saint John's Hospital in Santa Monica, where I immediately proceeded to the cafeteria and consumed one of the most delectable grilled cheese sandwiches I'd ever had. That should be another baby book instruction: eat a grilled cheese sandwich. I was supposed to be induced the next day at 8 a.m. My final words to Ed after saying, "Goodbye, have a good night, I love you" were, "Please don't be late."

What do you think?

He was running late.

Ed arrived about 9 a.m. That must have been close to eight o'clock in rock-star time. I was an hour into my Pitocin drip and experiencing contractions. He was fortunate that I was not armed. Ed was holding my hand and attempting to coach me over the final stretch nine hours later. But as he shouted "Push," I smelled peanuts on his breath. I was so hungry and in so much agony that the fragrance intensified. I recognized it right away as well. It was a PayDay candy bar, which was my favourite.

I couldn't believe his callous disregard. He couldn't do it, could he?

As it turned out, it was very simple.

He snuck out and scarfed down a PayDay a few minutes ago, while I was catching my breath between contractions. I didn't have time to whine any farther than I already had. Wolfie, weighing about eight pounds and measuring twenty-one inches in length, came at 6:56 p.m., and Ed switched from a candy bar to a cigar. The episode, however, was not forgotten. Wolfie, Ed, and I were celebrating Wolfie's birthday 27 years later. We reminisced and told stories over dinner. Then, as we were about to order dessert, Ed announced that he had a surprise for me. He reached inside his jacket pocket, grinning, and took out... guess what?

It's PayDay.

CHAPTER 4

THE WAY LEON LOOKS AT ME

DECEMBER 2019

I'm talking to Ed's helper, Leon, as he's resting in his hospital bed, recovering from the effects of a therapy. Leon is a clever, sophisticated young guy Ed met in Germany during one of his cancer treatment trips there. After becoming Ed's chef, Leon has evolved into a twenty-four-hour nurse-slash-caregiver, transporting him to appointments when Wolfie is unable, ensuring he takes his prescriptions on time, cooking his meals, and ensuring Ed has what he desires. I can see why they get along so well.

It's my first in-depth one-on-one conversation with Leon. He has travelled extensively and speaks four languages. He tells me about the meals he enjoys cooking for Ed. I tell stories about cooking for Ed after we were married and how Mrs. Van Halen taught me how to create his favourite dishes.

I tell Leon about my trip to Italy, where I fell in love with food all over again, and about Leon's gustatory excursions there, and soon Leon and I are discussing recipes, ingredients, and techniques with such passion that I almost forget we are in a hospital room with Ed.

"Edward told me that you have a cooking show on television," Leon explains.

"Yes, I have a lot of fun on it," I admit.

"It's fantastic that you enjoy food," he says.

I was maybe fifteen or sixteen years old at the time. I was ashamed because I thought I had an hourglass shape. I've always wished to be taller, blonder, and slimmer than I was. Every morning, I stepped on the scale, and the rest of the day was spent trying to make up for the result. I never considered eating out. I told myself to be careful. I was either awful, cheated, or slid at the conclusion of the day.

I despised going into the wardrobe for fittings on set. When they told me they needed to get a larger size for me, I wanted to die. I didn't understand they were bringing in small sizes since they assumed I was tiny, and the next sizes they got for me were still smalls. I assumed that the lower the number on the scale, the more attractive I was and the more employment I would receive. But it didn't work like that. I auditioned for the role of Lori Singer in the film Footloose, and when she got the job, I assumed it was because I wasn't as slim or as attractive as she was.

I was saddened when the same thing happened with the film Cocoon. I figured the casting directors thought I was unattractive and obese, or that something else was wrong with me. I never considered that I might not have been a good enough actor or that I might not have matched what they had in mind. I simply didn't grasp it.

I signed up to be a Jenny Craig spokesperson at the age of 47. I was open about my motivations. I declared to the world that I was fat— my weight was at an all-time high—and that my objective was to lose weight. Finally, That was exactly how I felt. I created an all-or-nothing situation in which the stakes were not only disappointment but also public embarrassment and disgrace if I didn't meet my goal, to say nothing of the emotional misery.

The plan reflected my mental state at the time: fractured, twisted, and unrealistic. I wasn't trying to lose weight or deal with the reasons for my weight gain over the years—the currents of misery, sadness, and discontent that ran beneath my outward smile. I wanted to lose weight. They are not the same thing.

But it also demonstrated my will to live. I divorced Ed in May of 2002 and refused to accept any money from him. I needed to make money as a single working mother. I couldn't find a job as an actress. Jenny Craig was a nice job, and it was going to help me lose weight. It was the finest of both worlds that mattered to me, and I gave everything I had to ensure my success.

The agreement required me to shed thirty pounds in eight months. I finished it in three days. Marc Schwartz, my manager, secured a new contract for ten pounds more. They asked if I would consider losing fifty pounds and posing in a bikini on the cover of People magazine after I shed the following 10 pounds faster than predicted. I agreed on the following terms: First, we avoided discussing the fifty pounds since I already knew it would be difficult to maintain such weight drop; and second, I wasn't going to try on said bikini until ten days before the scheduled photo session.

That entire time, I followed Jenny Craig's program as if I were a nun on a celibacy vow, which is how it felt at times. I ate pre-packaged meals, exercised, talked with my sponsor, and stepped on the scale for my weekly weigh-ins. The figures continued to fall. I was completely fatigued. I pretended to be in training. I was going to lose weight. I was going to have the body I had always desired.

The bikini photo session was set to take place around the end of March 2009. My manager had contacted me in the morning ten days previously.

He said, "How are you feeling?"

"Let's do it," I said.

I didn't eat much over the next week and a half. I wanted to put on that bikini and show off my abs and definition, so I did. The photo shoot was conducted in complete secrecy. No one on the set was permitted to bring their phone. A week later, I appeared on the cover of People magazine sporting a tiny green bikini (which, by the way, was a large—even at my tiniest, 122 pounds, I still wore a large, demonstrating how messed-up the fashion industry's sizing is). A Jenny Craig commercial was also on repeat.

"Now nothing's stopping me from diving into summer," I remarked as I completed a backflip into a pool.

My grin was genuine. The splash was genuine. I was overjoyed. I demonstrated that if I set my mind to it, I could accomplish anything—and I was slim.

CHAPTER 5

SECRET INGREDIENTS

APRIL 2020

On my sixty-first birthday, I get up at three-thirty a.m. to prepare for an appearance on the Today show. I wash my face, brush my hair, dress professionally, and pour coffee into my eyes. Or it appears that I did. On the West Coast, it is still early. The show commemorated by sending me two rosemary plants, two lavender plants, and two massive floral bouquets—one for each decade. I'm live on the air with Hoda, Savannah, and Carson at a little after five a.m. I pop open a bottle of my favourite champagne, which they also sent, and raise a virtual glass to everyone.

I joke that it's too early to drink, and at that hour, it does sound a little crazy, but as we laugh, I remember times when I was on the road with Ed and we rolled into our hotel room about this time and had just one more. I wasn't always the stereotypical goody-two-shoes. In fact, once I'm off the air, I tell myself, "What the hell, you're only sixty once," and take a taste of champagne.

Woo-hoo. It was a wild ride. Par-tee.

The girl still has it.

The girl then changes back into her T-shirt and sweatpants and returns to bed. I have no reservations about reaching this milestone. I've been thinking about it more and more as the actual date, April 23, approaches. Sixty sounded older and more AARP-worthy than fifty-nine, which had its own importance, like waiting in traffic to turn left from one period of life into another. I was more concerned with how I might feel than with how I actually felt during the day.

After I wake up, I spend the day doing nothing. I peruse the paper and take another drink of coffee. My favourite muffins are blueberry, banana, and oat. I adore muffins, particularly these, and the delightful aroma from the oven transports me back to my youth, when my mother baked blueberry muffins or banana bread and I waited in the kitchen, anticipating the first mouthful of those newly created, warm goodies. I'm ten years old all over again. Of course, I use fresh blueberries and bananas, but when I make this batch, the liberal splash of vanilla in the recipe sticks out to me as a critical element, almost a secret ingredient that gives the muffins their taste. Or, if it isn't fully responsible for the flavour, it enriches it in the same way that butter finishes off pasta sauce, lemon sprinkled on top of a melon brings out the luxuriant juices, and rosemary in vegetables transforms every bite into a garden celebration.

"There are no such things as secrets in the kitchen," observed the late, great LA chef Michael Roberts, whose restaurant, Trumps, was an institution on par with Spago in the 1980s. "However, there are secret ingredients, which are not tasted but would be missed if they were omitted." "A secret ingredient is one that enhances the flavour of a dish without drawing attention to itself."

I approach each birthday in the same way: by including the hidden components. I'm going for a walk. I take a deep breath and smell the roses. I snipped some flowers. Spring has arrived. Wolfie comes by but remains in the backyard because of Covid-19. I ran into him out there. It's strange, bizarre, and sad, especially since I don't get a hug from him or anyone else. I respond to birthday texts from people I would typically see on my birthday, telling myself to embrace the love they are sending me. My closest buddies send over food from one of our favourite restaurants—the French bistro where we would have congregated if the virus-inspired lockdown hadn't occurred— and we dine together over Zoom at night. It's not the same as being there in person, but we make the most of it by telling stories and laughing for a few hours. I didn't spend time with girlfriends in my twenties, and I didn't have any at the time. Ed and all of the techs, engineers, and musicians who worked with him in the studio and on tour were always around me. It reminded me of a Scout unit from the dark side of the moon.

But tonight is yet another example of how my girlfriends have assisted me in creating new memories. We've supported each other up through large and minor life milestones, such as health concerns, birthdays, anniversaries, job changes, career decisions, elections, and now a pandemic. We bring a lot of shared history to the table—or, in this case, to Zoom—and the experience never disappoints. I gain insights and understanding that I would not have had otherwise, and for however long we are together—tonight it's for a couple of hours—I rarely think about myself, at least not in the brooding, judgmental way that I do when I am alone. Instead, I give, share, and serve—whether it be food, an opinion, encouragement, support, guidance, or humour. Remember the children's book The Giving Tree by author Shel Silverstein? It's about a tree who adored a young boy more than she adored herself. It concludes with both of them having gotten older, the youngster becoming an old man in need of a place to sit and relax and the tree being little more than a stump but still ready to assist him in some manner. "Come on, Boy, take a seat." "Sit down and relax," she advises. "And the youngster did. And the tree was overjoyed."

This is at the heart of my passion for cooking. Over the last decade, I've changed my connection with food, first with a trip to Italy, then with a cookbook, and now with a TV series, and I've reconnected with principles that are essential to me. My cooking is driven by a love of the process: selecting ingredients, creating something new and wonderful, and then sharing it with others. When you're stuck in a dieting rut, you don't eat with other people. You cannot have connections during mealtime. You are separating yourself from food, other people, yourself, and life. Cooking gave me the opportunity to reconnect with all I had denied myself and missed. It's a daily struggle since old negative habits are difficult to break, but I try and try and try, and when I succeed, like Shel Silverstein's giving tree, I'm overjoyed.

Someone inquired as to what I desired for my birthday. Here's what I'm looking for:

I want to be able to laugh like Julia Roberts, a joyful, heartfelt laugh that emerges from within and rocks the entire room.

I want my child to be happy and healthy.

I want the same thing for my brothers and their spouses and children, as well as my friends and their families.

I want people, especially children, to have enough to eat and drink.

I want plenty of whatever people need to spread around so that everyone receives their fair share. That's all.

What makes me nervous about turning sixty? It's getting closer to eighty, and I believe that's when I'll die. Let me clarify.

Ed and I attended a party at singer Sammy Hagar's house many years ago. He was living near us at the beach at the time. There was a psychic at the party who I had seen privately about a year before for weight loss advice. I was 136 pounds at the time and thought I needed to shed 10 pounds, which was a sure sign of madness. But I was visiting a psychic for diet guidance, so that was enough. The psychic began by inquiring as to what I had for breakfast. When I informed him I had an English muffin with peanut butter, he trembled and moved away from me, as if hearing it had given him a terrifying vision.

"No, no, no, Valerie," he chastised. "You can't do it." It sets the tone for the rest of the day."

I should have asked who was telling him that—was it his opinion or someone on the other side, and if so, who was it, because the women on my side of the family who might have been hovering around him would have said that this wasn't enough and would have encouraged me to eat even more. Nonetheless, I trusted him. Breakfast became coffee, and I was overjoyed when we ran into each other again at Sammy's. We found a quiet spot to sit and he read to me again. This one, for whatever reason, was concerned with life and longevity. During the reading, he casually stated that I will die in my early eighties and Ed would die in his mid-sixties. I never forgot what he said, possibly because he was so explicit, or perhaps because we all wonder how long this unfathomable miracle of our existence will last.

After both of my parents died, three years apart but at the same age of eighty-two, I remembered his reading. Ed, who had reached sixty-five in January, didn't appear to be on his way out, but he wasn't having an easy time either.

It got me thinking. What would I want to do if I only had twenty years left? Why should it be limited to twenty years? What if I just had one day? Or how about an hour? What would I like to accomplish right now? The solution came to me in an instant. I'd like to stop squandering my time. I want to appreciate myself. I want to get off the treadmill of self-hatred. I want to be able to forgive myself for my slips and tears, as well as the times when I don't feel strong, loving, or kind. I want to be able to notice and enjoy life's small pleasures when they arise. I want to give myself permission to always be myself, no matter what that looks or feels like at this age.

The finest part about being sixty is being able to say, "Enough already," and mean it. The number is no longer relevant. It is the sensation that is important. What am I thinking? What effect am I having on others? I've spent my entire life being told to get out of my comfort zone. I don't want to leave now. I want to spend the rest of my life as author Anne Lamott outlined in her book Plan B: A Year of Discontent. Additional Thoughts on Faith: "Age has provided me with what I've been looking for my entire life—it has provided me with me." It has given me time, experience, mistakes, and victories, as well as time-tested friends who have assisted me in stepping into the shape that was waiting for me. "I now fit into myself." And guess what? That is the exact size I want to feel at ease in—me.

The question is, how do you go about doing this? I say things like, "I want to be kinder and more loving to myself," as do so many other people, as if it's as simple as flipping a switch and becoming that person in seven steps. It is not the case. What I've discovered since saying, "Enough already," a few months ago is that it takes effort. Every day, I have to remind myself that the way I want to love myself and experience joy is a value and a purpose that I must continually realign with.

What I'm learning, relearning, and continuously telling myself is that joy, happiness, gratitude, and all the other things we all seek, including love, will not find me. I'll have to go out and look for them. Every one of us does. That is how it is for everyone.

The good news is that there is just one step to being kinder and more loving, rather than seven, fifteen, or an entire how-to book: simply follow your heart.

You simply do it. You go with your gut instinct.

When you allow it, your heart will always bring you to the same place: one of helping, giving, and being kind. This is something I do with food. I enjoy feeding people. It warms my heart. I wish I had pushed myself in this direction a long time ago—away from the scale and the mirror and toward feeding people. I should have known better. However, the experience never fails to return the warmth and love that I wish to feel for myself. It allows me to see the version of myself that I prefer. I never try to fix myself because a part of me doesn't believe it needs mending. It's caring and kind, and it shows that the most important part of me, my heart, isn't broken. I'd been on lockdown for a month and a half by my birthday. I despise Covid's treatment of us. Everyone I know is perplexed, terrified, irritated, searching for answers, and hoping for the best. I'd want to invite them over and prepare a meal for them.

CHAPTER 6

NO TIME LIKE TODAY

MAY 2020

I have some advice for everyone who feels compelled to contact someone important in their life, whether it's a parent, an aunt or uncle, your ex, a former neighbour or teammate, a teacher or colleague: Do it. Make the call, send the email, or write the DM based on your instincts. There is no better moment than now.

Although your mind is not always sensible, your heart is never wrong. This is because I'm having difficulty getting together with Ed. I'm irritated. We shouldn't have any trouble seeing each other because we're in constant communication and routinely check in via text. It began in November of last year, when I was in New York promoting Valerie's Home Cooking. I FaceTimed with Wolfie while shopping at the Nintendo store to show him all the wonderful Zelda merchandise they had, then on the way out, I noticed the giant tree at Rockefeller Center, which reminded me of Ed.

I call him, and he answers. I tell him where I am and that I am wandering alone around Midtown Manhattan. The last time the three of us were in New York together was on Van Halen's 2015 tour. We didn't spend much time together, but we had a good time, and Ed and I talked about it even if there wasn't much to say.

"I just wanted to let you know I was thinking about you," I explained.

"Thanks. Have a wonderful time for me there."

"I will. "I adore you."

"I adore you as well."

We want to get together over the next few months but can't seem to make it work except while Ed is in the hospital in January. Then I start working on my show, Covid arrives, and I'm too worried about carrying the virus into his house and making him sick, despite the fact that I tested negative throughout the spring. We're still texting. It's mostly mundane. One day, he asks, "So, what shows are you watching?" I mail him a couple books. "Thanks a lot, Val." Otherwise, I simply check in with no answer required. "I'm thinking of you." "I hope your day is going well."

Ed and I divorced twenty years ago. People are constantly amazed at how close we have stayed. I, too, am struck by how much affection we still have for each other, given how badly we harmed each other years ago. But we grew up and moved on, and motherhood and the love we've always had for each other proved to be more powerful and resilient than anything else. We opted to stay friends and family—and we worked hard to do so.

We got through hard spots with therapy, but we always knew we didn't want to go through life apart. Second marriages were included in this category. I was on the groom's side when Ed married publicist Janie Liszewski in 2009. Ed and Janie were present for my wedding to Tom the following year to toast our I dos. Ironically, both of our marriages are currently in disarray. I haven't told him about Tom and me, and while Ed suggested that he was probably on the verge of divorce, I wasn't going to ask him for specifics. If I had been more curious, I would have visited him more frequently over the last few months to drop off meals, watch TV, or simply keep him company.

It breaks my heart to think he was alone or lonely. Meanwhile, I couldn't decide whether it would be wrong to serve him pasta or watch a football game with him. Now I'm thinking, "Really, Val?" What is it like to call and inquire, "How ya doin'?" "Are you hungry?" "Can I make you something?" isn't it? That afternoon in 2018, when Ed and I crossed paths at the studio where Wolfie was rehearsing with his band, I should have learned my lesson. When Ed came, I was already there. He greeted me with a kiss and sat on a nearby sofa. My heart prompted me to go up, sit next to him, and wrap my arm around him so we could both be proud parents.

Just go ahead and do it, I told myself. But I refused to budge. Not right now. Even though I was the only one who saw the boundaries, I was afraid to cross them. It may be said that I was getting in my own way... again. I eventually got closer to him, and I'm pleased I did. Ed not only appreciated the company, but when I asked how he was doing, he had bad news: his illness had gone to his brain. I was stunned and paralyzed as I glanced at him.

What?

"Yeah," he answered, his gaze fixed on the floor, as though he couldn't believe what a massive bummer had been dealt to him yet again.

He went on to say that he had crashed his motorcycle on Mulholland Drive and that an examination had revealed the outcomes. I saw that I had placed my arm across his knees as he told me the information. It was something I had done without thinking as a means of being close, but when I saw it, I immediately thought, Uh-oh, this is kind of intimate. It was intimate—and entirely fitting for the situation. So was the way I encircled him and squeezed as firmly as I could, attempting to express everything that was so difficult at the time: love, strength, and hope.

My ideas about what was appropriate were illogical. There's nothing wrong with telling someone you love them. Period.

I was grateful for Ed and I having our time a year later in George Lopez's car on Thanksgiving, and I was a little more relaxed about seeing him after that, though we still missed opportunities to be together. One SMS exchange in particular is excruciating. We were planning to meet up for Thursday night football. I was going to prepare dinner for us. But that morning, I received a text from Ed recommending that we reschedule.

"Let me go through today's radiation treatment first because I don't know how I'm going to feel afterward," he wrote. "Usually it's pretty shitty."

I understood, wished him well, and informed him that I hadn't yet gone shopping for ingredients, so we could reschedule whenever he was available.

Ed emailed me later that afternoon to tell me that the machine had broken down and that he wouldn't be able to obtain the treatment in time for me to come over and watch the game. I offered another date because it was late and I was focused on bringing over food but hadn't gone to the supermarket. I wish I hadn't made seeing him a condition of dinner and instead simply went over there and hung around for an hour. In actuality, neither of us was concerned with supper as much as we were with spending time together. We, like so many others, were unable to articulate ourselves clearly.

He has continued to give opportunities to hang out since then. He has informed me that he is resuming his football career. He's inquired as to what shows I'm viewing. But, for some reason, I keep putting up hurdles, fretting about making the incorrect impression, then beating myself up for overthinking things and wasting precious time we could spend together.

My life story. I declined job interviews because I didn't want people to see me at my current weight. Because I thought I was obese, I stayed in my bedroom for days and weeks. Because I was trying to be decent, I declined dinner invites from pals. And I'm wondering why I'm so desperate for joy and happiness.

How much time did I waste dieting to drop ten pounds? We have no business treating time as if it were infinite and would always be there, like a half-empty jar of pickle relish on a refrigerator shelf. For me, waste has always been defined by those ten pounds. Losing 10 pounds would make me happy, prettier, more fulfilled, and finished. It took over my life. It still does on occasion. But when I look back at images of myself at fifty, forty, sixteen, or any other age, I wonder, "What were you thinking?" What a squandering of time.

And it was never the ten pounds that were the issue.

So, what exactly do those 10 pounds represent?

I didn't treat myself any better when I shed those ten pounds. The 10 pounds were insufficient. Which begs the question, what will suffice? How about a grand total of £500? Please do not laugh. Everyone who has ever assessed their happiness on a scale should consider this: I've been trying for forty years to shed ten pounds. I've gained and lost. Sometimes there is more, sometimes there is less. At the very least, that amounts to £400, and it hasn't been enough, which is insane. It's similar to a dog chasing its tail. There is no ultimate goal. It's a crazy, tiring, never-ending circle.

Because it's never been about the scale. Every time I've mentioned wanting or needing to drop those ten pounds, it symbolises something else going on in my life, something that's making me sad, hurting me, or making me worry. It may have been a party I hoped to get invited to or a school test I hoped to ace when I was a teenager. Later, I might have been worried about something at work, such as clothes I wanted to wear or a part I wanted to get. It was my rage and insecurity while I was married to Ed. I gained weight after losing both of my parents within three years, and instead of addressing my loss and despair, I focused on the food I was eating and everything I stated I couldn't eat.

And now it's Ed's turn.

It's because I'm worried about my son.

It's my personal fear of losing someone whose presence in my life has been so important that I can't picture living without him.

When I ask myself why I can't lose weight, I'm really wondering why I can't get a hold of myself. Why am I ignoring what is truly bothering me? Instead, the emphasis is always on those ten pounds because that figure, as well as the weight itself, is something I can target and ostensibly control through willpower. I'll lose weight if I adjust my eating habits. And losing weight will make me feel better.

I will be able to eliminate the problem or difficulties that I am not now addressing.

But that is the wrong approach. When you consider how the emotions, tension, fears, and anxieties that we carry about with us may seem like weight, you begin to not just understand but also experience what those ten pounds really mean. Losing weight is a means of appearing to manage and control situations that appear to be unmanageable and uncontrollable otherwise. However, it does not function. I can't tell you how many times I've convinced myself that if I simply lost 10 pounds, I'll feel better about everything. It appears to be concrete, doable, and simple. It only costs ten pounds. Who says you can't lose ten pounds?

My hand is raised.

Here's the issue. Trying to lose 10 pounds or any other amount of pounds does not address the underlying issues, and there is always something else, some other issue, and thus there are another ten pounds that you or I decide we need to drop. Dieting may assist us in fitting into a smaller pair of jeans, but it will not assist us in fitting into our lives. Believe me. Take a look at me. I know exactly what I'm talking about.

The idea is to live in the present moment rather than on the scale. Remind yourself that it's not the weight, and it never has been. It isn't 10 pounds. It's the troubles that come with that ten pounds. I see someone who is a touch heavy in the mirror these days, but what I truly see is grief and sadness that I haven't dealt with. I'm not going to be able to lose those. I have to work through them, and when I do, I believe there is a good chance that the weight will follow.

Take a deep breath, I tell myself. Gather the confidence to face the true difficulties, the sorrow, anguish, despair, regrets, and fear. Discuss them. Allow yourself to cry if you need to. Forgive yourself for any errors you've made. Then, try your best to push through them and ahead, knowing that this is the only road to a better, healthier, and happier you.

And don't put it off any longer. Today is the day.

CHAPTER 7

A ROOM WITH A VIEW

LATE SPRING–SUMMER 2020

I've never been one of those individuals who decorates their home like a museum or a movie set, with each object carefully selected to seem camera-ready in case Architectural Digest unexpectedly comes on the door for a photo shoot. My home is clearly and purposefully comfy. I blame my upbringing. Some folks are overly formal. I'm not. I grew up wearing flip-flops, faded blue jeans, and T-shirts (the one I'm wearing now is bleached maroon with the word PEACE across the front), and my home has the same laid-back vibe.

My pets and dog are free to roam the premises. My grown-up child still shows up with buddies, expecting me to have a well-stocked fridge. Most days, I work at the kitchen table, which is piled high with recipes, magazines, newspaper clippings, notes, mail, reminders, to-do lists, and other evidence that I operate at a slower pace than the rest of the world.

I prefer to travel at my own leisure. I attempted the fast lane in my twenties. Since then, I've learned that I'm much better at driving on the left side of the road. Actually, I'm at my best when the car is in the garage and I can be right here at home, which, I've realised, is a project that parallels the work I've done (or haven't done) and continue to do on myself. It hasn't been without hassles and procrastination, deliberation and expenditure, but I've arrived at a point where I really, really enjoy myself.

Some people do this with their homes, gardens, or automobiles—something that expresses who they are at the time and the work they are always doing on themselves. Ed is like that; in addition to his musical talent, he has the mentality of an engineer. He's often referred to himself as a tinkerer, a skilled do-it-yourself trait he received from his father, who was also a musician. Mr. Van Halen played the clarinet and saxophone, and once had to modify the latter after losing a finger while attempting to lift a neighbour's U-Haul trailer off its jacks and out of his way at three a.m.

Please do not inquire. It's classic Van Halen family lore—equal parts machismo, booze, and inventiveness. Maybe not in equal parts. Ed began constructing and dismantling guitars in high school. He is the holder of two US patents, 4656917 and 388117. The first was for a smoother neck that would allow him to play his distinctive tapping method, and the second was for a better guitar peghead that would make restringing easier. He wrote about both in Popular Mechanics in 2015. He had a workshop in his studio that looked like it belonged on This Old House; it was so packed with dozens of projects in various stages that he could have had his own show called This Old Guitar. He kept everything and could tell you how many drops of 3-IN-ONE oil he put in the nut of a whammy bar he repaired in the 1970s.

I recall him giving a tour of the studio during an MTV News interview with Chris Connelly in the late 1990s. We hadn't yet broken up, and I recall fondly the 5150 studio. It looked like one of those locations from American Pickers where things are heaped floor to ceiling and only the owner knows where they are. He had built a racquetball court and turned it into his personal playhouse to get past the local rules. As he gave Chris the tour, they came across shelves of tapes, what appeared to be hundreds of them, containing at least hundreds of hours of music, if not a lifetime of music.

Ed added, laughing, that all the tapes had been numbered and the contents catalogued on a broken-down Radio Shack computer. Attempts to recover the information were all futile. Ed claimed to be the only person who could index what was on them. He remembered taking out a tape from 1983 with the song "Right Now" on it; that classic was released eight years later, in 1991. He shrugged and said he'd look through them someday.

I'm not sure if that day ever came. But Ed's persistent pursuit of perfection—whether in music, on his instruments, or remembering what he'd made and figuring out how and when to apply it—has motivated and defined him for as long as I've known him, and it was that way before I met him.

My mother was like that, but in a different way. She was a fantastic artist, a painter who got lost in her canvases. She worked as a travel agent after all of us kids had grown up, which was similar to painting landscapes. She enjoyed assisting people in planning their vacations. She listened to their reasons for travelling: some were for work, some were for family holidays, and some were much-needed escapes during times of crisis. I believe her work, like her art, served as a therapeutic getaway, allowing her to enter a place where she eventually came to grips with the sadness of losing her second-born child. My house has served as a conduit for me to enter myself. For nearly two decades, it has mirrored who I am at the time and allowed me to reinvent, correct, and alter. It has evolved into a spot where I can unwind and enjoy my surroundings. It has reminded me of my own strength. It's allowed me to see myself as a work in progress. It has taught me when something has to be fixed and when I should stop and absorb beauty. It has given me roots as well as the confidence to demolish and rebuild. It has given me perspective.

It does not have to be a residence. It could be just one room. An automobile, a park bench, a public garden, a guitar, or a picture are all examples. It was my home for me. We literally evolved into one another. After deciding to leave Ed, I started looking at houses. Our property and assets were divided amicably and easily. Finding a new place to live was not easy. Every day, I drove around the surrounding communities, seeking FOR SALE signs. I had several fundamental requirements, beginning with budget and location. I had a spending plan. For Wolfie's sake, I wanted to be close to Ed. I wanted to be near Wolfie's school. And I desired seclusion.

Then I looked for intangibles, those enigmatic traits in a home that welcomed me in and promised comfort. The house I had left was a fantasy. I had worked with architects to design what Ed and I had envisioned: adequate bedrooms for three to four kids, plenty of closet space, and enough space for our hectic lives. We had so much space that we had separate lives. Now all I needed was a place to settle in, gather my thoughts, figure out what was next, and help raise my child.

While driving through the hills somewhat east of Ed's property, I came across the house that would become mine. I'd passed Coldwater and Laurel Canyons, exited Mulholland Drive, and was aimlessly drifting down little winding lanes when I noticed a tree on a hill. I couldn't make out the house. However, the tree turned out to be a large, solid live oak with sweeping limbs that, upon closer inspection, appeared to be accessible and offering a lift up, which was exactly what I needed. I also imagined Wolfie having a great time climbing the tree. I believe he climbed it twice. Nonetheless, I purchased the tree and stayed for the house. The house, like me, was in rough shape. Water had caused damage. Decks were shattered. The stairs were shaky. There were three porches: one off the kitchen, one off the living room, and one off the TV room, all of which were in various states of disrepair. The house featured four bedrooms, two on each side, and I liked that Wolfie and I could sleep in one end of the house while I used the other as an office and a guest room. The kitchen, on the other hand, made me feel like this was going to be my new home. It was right in the middle of the home, which made sense to me. What was more important in everyday life than a kitchen?

Though it hadn't been transformed into one of those gleaming industrial offices with a farmhouse patina that were so trendy at the time, it was spacious and cosy, and reminded me immediately of the kind of kitchen my Nonnie and Aunt Adeline would approve of. The appliances were organised neatly around a wide centre island; I imagined the two of them kneading out pasta dough there, just like they did in my Aunt Adeline's basement in Delaware. Later on, I'd cook there with my mother. I'm not sure if the best decisions are made in the gut, but the tastiest are.

I was certain about one thing: the enormous picture window at the far end of the kitchen. The house was perched on a hill, and the view out that window seemed to go on forever. I could see the homes and stores below, the freeway traffic, the Burbank skyline, planes flying to Bob Hope Airport, and the mountains in the distance as I looked across the valley. The stars hovered like goodies in a cosmic pantry as light streamed through the glass at night. I needed the light, the stars, the perspective, and everything in between.

Ed was the first person I showed it to. I wanted him to see that Wolfie and I were safe. He approved and gave me a thumbs up.

We moved in and lived in the house for nearly five years before I began to seriously consider making modifications. It reminded me of my own life, how I acquired weight, stewed over it for years, and gained even more weight until I finally signed up for Jenny Craig. I felt the same way about the house. I noticed the deck deteriorating and made a mental note to take care of it, but three years later it had been eaten away by dry rot and bugs to the point that I couldn't stand on it without risking harm.

As I strolled around the backyard one day, I realised I'd had enough of this obstacle course. I made the decision to act. If I'm going to fix one deck, I might as well fix them all, I reasoned. It turned out to be the season for repairs. Ed and I divorced so that he could remarry. Tom and I got engaged and decided to organise our own wedding. Wolfie joined Van Halen on the road. With so much going on, why not remodel the entire house?

That's how I roll. Delay till the small things add up to the big picture. However, change generates its own momentum, and I was caught up in the possibility and excitement. I discussed with my architect the possibility of constructing an upstairs master bedroom—my eagle's nest—to take advantage of the vista and renovating the swimming pool. I was happy with the living and dining rooms as they were, but I saw an opportunity to expand the kitchen and replace the cupboards and appliances to create the type of cooking environment I'd always wanted.

Everything felt right, like a natural progression. The decks were about putting myself on solid ground. The second-story bedroom was all about freeing my spirit. It was all about nourishing my spirit in the kitchen. And the swimming pool, which I found myself enjoying in my fantasies, represented a new beginning for myself.

One piece of the puzzle had me baffled. That was my closet in my bedroom. I thought I wanted a spacious new closet, one of those secret apartment-style closets I saw in magazines. When you opened the door, you were greeted by an oasis of opulence and organisation. Was it, however, me? I am not a consumer. I prefer T-shirts and jeans. Maybe I should conduct a huge purge of what I have and start again with a more modest wardrobe. I could construct a meditation nook. A coffee shop on the second floor. A reading nook.

Then I spotted my Wallabees and put an end to all fifty of my fancies. What was I thinking? I was a slacker. I also saw the knee-high silver platform boots I wore in the One Day at a Time episode in which Mackenzie and I dressed up as Elton John and Kiki Dee and sang "Don't Go Breaking My Heart." I closed the closet doors and contacted my architect, despite the fact that I hadn't worn those boots since we shot that episode in 1976. "Ignore what I just stated. The closet must be spacious."

Following the airing of the One Day show, Elton sent me an autographed photograph in which he stated that I was a better Elton

John than he was. It's been reframed twice. It's one of my most prized possessions. So it's possible that I'm just a big old softie rather than a hoarder. But one thing remained constant about me. I continued to proceed at my own pace. For almost three years, the blueprints for all of this sat on my dining-room table.

Finally, we broke ground, and I was ecstatic, but what I remember most about the early days of construction is that we moved out to the beach house I bought in the 1980s, and for the next two years, I had an hour-and-a-half commute twice a day from there to the studio where we shot Hot in Cleveland, despite the fact that my real house was exactly one mile—or about ten minutes—from the set.

I suppose it added to the suspense.

I had two additions as the process progressed. I desired a productive and edible garden. I yearned for the one I'd had at Ed's. I was quite picky. I imagined a plethora of fruit trees, including orange, lemon, lime, grapefruit, guava, kumquat, avocado, and whatever other trees my brilliant gardener, Carlos, felt would flourish. I also imagined veggies, rosemary hedges, and herb clusters.

I found myself, like my mother and Ed, tinkering with the yard. I was finally coming out of my depression at the breakup of my first marriage and the following uncertainty about who I was supposed to be at this point in my life, and the garden mirrored this. It was significant to me. I was prepared to be fertile, fruitful, nourishing, and new—all of the qualities I observed in a garden. I was also prepared to embark on a new relationship with food. Instead of avoiding it, I wanted to nurture it. I wanted to be a part of the process. I had travelled to Italy. I'd created a cookbook. I'd fallen in love with relishing every aspect of a meal.

I didn't simply eat the components; I savoured them as well. I didn't need to know where my carrots and peas came from, but I did want to appreciate the freshness and attention that went into making the food. I saw myself gathering the bounty from my garden, bringing it inside, and creating simple but tasty foods for family and friends.

Dieting was not on my mind; but, doing something creative, warm, and personal was. This was not about restriction or denial; rather, it was about reaching forward and accepting something I had previously deemed terrible or off-limits. I wasn't even aware of the change. I was acting instinctively. My body wanted me to eat, but my soul wanted me to grow.

It took several years to plant the garden and even longer before it began producing abundant fruit and vegetables. That was a nice thing to happen. I needed to practise patience and get into the habit of giving the garden daily attention and care, which was something I also needed to work on with myself. That was and still is the most important takeaway.

Happiness and joy are the benefits of a healthy life, but they require daily effort. This is something that my garden reminds me of. You must get your hands filthy. A library was another aspect I kept an eye on while it was being built. This room, more than the shattered decks, may have spurred the entire remodel. The library is actually a nook with floor-to-almost-ceiling bookcases and a comfy chair where I can plant my butt and read while gazing out at the gorgeous vista. It's a nice, comfy hideaway where I can appreciate the silence, tranquillity, and magic of simply being.

I have meditation friends. They persuaded me to get a meditation chair. I did, and it now serves as a landing area for sweaters and T-shirts in my bedroom. When I look up from a book or a crossword puzzle and gaze out the window for five, 10, or even twenty minutes, I am meditating. As I filter through a million different thoughts, I finally find myself thinking about how lovely everything is until I realise I've cleaned my mind and am thinking of nothing. I've seen birds soar and the sky fill with smoke from uncontrolled flames. I've flown across the sky on fluffy clouds, spying deer eating in my prized garden.

I've sat here thinking about my parents as they aged and eventually died of illnesses. I could feel their presence long after they were gone. I've been thinking about my late brother. I imagined him as a toddler, despite the fact that I never met him. I've been thinking about my own son as he's gotten older, graduated, and moved out on his own. I've laughed, cried, and been concerned. I've pondered my own good fortune and all the blessings that surround me, and I've questioned why I still struggle to feel good about myself. I've been thinking about Ed and his disease. I've prayed to the sky both throughout the day and at night for him to survive. I questioned God about it.

I've been thinking lately about what might come next, what that will be like for Ed, Wolfie, and all of us. How will that feel? What will it be like? I've looked to the clouds and the stars for answers. I looked through the mountains and the woods. I've seen them change and felt the ageless nature of the broader picture. I've noticed how we pass through as visitors, and how seeing ourselves in that light prioritises and reprioritized things.

I sit here marvelling at the world's beauty and imperfections, and I think I need to start looking at myself in the same way: with respect and admiration for all of the parts in the amazing jigsaw that is me and my life, including those that don't seem to fit. I've arrived at the conclusion that having a room with a view is necessary for happiness. However, you do not require one like mine. Everyone has one of their own. It's known as the human heart. A full, warm, forgiving, aching, healing, and loving heart is the best window through which to see yourself and the world. I was thinking the other day about a secret little nook in the garden near the oak tree where I installed a bench. I haven't sat on it in months, but I like knowing it's there, waiting for me to arrive, like I've been doing for much of my life.

I'm making progress. Definitely. I'm making progress.

CHAPTER 8

THE TWENTY-ONE GRAM DIET

MARCH 2020

I just ended a question-and-answer session with a fourth-grade class. My co-hosting duties on the Food Network's youngsters Baking Championship have made me popular with this age group, and I have given these youngsters freedom to ask me whatever question they want. The first question, however—"What four adjectives best describe you?"—made me wish I hadn't been so careless about the defining limits.

Please do not laugh. The issue was that I couldn't tell the difference between an adjective and an adverb.

That was nothing compared to when a female asked me what made me happy. Leave it to a child to get right to the point.

"Well, shoot," I couldn't reply, "I've been asking myself that same question for years, especially lately." But I came really close. I contemplated explaining that these things seemed to have altered depending on my age, whether I was nine years old like them, in my twenties or thirties, or sixty years old. However, as I considered various responses, I realised that the things that truly make me happy haven't changed over the years: a hug from my son, a grilled cheese sandwich on a rainy day, reading a good book, seeing one of my cats napping on the windowsill, pretty flowers, falling asleep outside while reading, the fresh air in spring and fall, a walk along the beach, laughing until I need to go to the bathroom...

If anything, I said to the kids, the list has grown to include watching my son in love, receiving a surprise text from Ed, feeling healthy, learning a new tip or trick from one of my phenomenally skilled chef friends, and other such things.

Later on, I realised I didn't specify that being skinny or weighing less made me happy. It never occurred to me. What do you think about that? I believe it is food for thinking. Years of dieting and cleansing have left me hungry, and what I'm looking for isn't in the fridge or cupboard. What I desire is to be fed compassion, forgiveness, gratitude, kindness, and love. This is what I mean when I say that the joy I want to feel is not so much an end goal as it is a value and an aim that I must constantly realign with.

Joy is not going to find me. Every day, I have to actively pursue it. I realise I'm repeating myself. But that is all that is required. Constant nagging. Joy, contentment, and thankfulness must be sought after. They don't just come across us. We must locate them. I have the same feelings about feeding my spirit. I have to be deliberate about it. Every single day. The way I try to sit in the sun for a few minutes with a book, or look out my kitchen window at the vista and wonder at the beauty of the mountains in the distance, or literally pause to smell the roses. This is spiritual nourishment. It's necessary for my health. I believe it is something that we all require and desire.

What happened to this diet? Where can we find a simple recipe for feeding our souls so that our stomachs don't continuously tell us we're hungry? How can we eat to feel good rather than to avoid feeling?

I've devised a seven-day program to nourish the soul. It's called the 21-Gram Diet. We purportedly weigh twenty-one grams less after we die than while our hearts were still pumping blood to our extremities and our bodies were still breathing. The weight of our soul is supposed to be twenty-one grams. This has assisted me in coming to the following important realisation: no matter how much weight I shed, I still feel heavy. But when my soul is fed, I feel lighter regardless of the number on the scale.

So, have I, and everyone else who has begun a diet or cleanse, gone about it incorrectly? Have we been indoctrinated to disregard logic? Shouldn't we be feeding our souls rather than striving to lose weight?

Consider the following: A little puppy, a compact microwave, a bowling ball, a large bag of sugar, a sack of potatoes, and three two-litre bottles of Pepsi all weigh 10 pounds. A paper clip, a quarter teaspoon of sugar, a thumbtack, a piece of gum, and any US banknote all weigh one gram. It should be simpler to add a paperclip than it should be to lose a tiny microwave.

This is not a substitute for morning affirmations, ten-minute sun salutations, breathing exercises, stretching, yoga, meditation, absorbing crystal energy, or pampering yourself silly by starting your day with a beautiful omelette if that's what you're into. Go ahead and forgo dessert or yell at or with Rachel Maddow. I'm not trying to get in the way. What I'm saying is that you include this diet into your regular routine. Set up at least a few minutes each day for this diet, just as you would for your vitamins. You can devote more time to it if you have the time, but remember that the purpose is to fill your soul.

Day One: Permission

Give yourself permission to feel happy and notice all your fantastic, amazing, and positive traits on the first day of the Twenty-One Gram Diet, rather than focusing on what you consider faults, flaws, and imperfections. Allow yourself to switch off the news and watch something you enjoy instead. Allow yourself to listen to music, go for a stroll, call a friend, read a nice book, or even a trashy magazine. Allow yourself to venture outside of your comfort zone and do something insane. Alternatively, give yourself permission to curl up inside your comfort zone and relax. Allow oneself to expand rather than contract.

Day Two: Compassion

Recognize the hardship and suffering you have undergone for years on the second day. The battle to feel good about yourself and perceive yourself as unique and lovely and deserving of love and compassion is real, especially if you've spent years, if not your entire life, telling yourself that you're not worthy or a failure or categorising yourself as bad, obese, ugly, or unlovable. The agony is palpable. Recognize it. If you need to, cry. Return to the source of the problem. You may not have told anyone about it, but you are aware of its existence. Or perhaps you don't know what it is, but the sensation is there. Play it back in your head. Look at yourself. Look at the situation to see what it was. Recognize that you have spent your entire life evaluating yourself as a result of it. This decision has influenced your actions. It hasn't just been bad for you. It has also been cruel, needless, and ineffective. Say, "Enough already." In the future, treat yourself with care and recognize that you are not perfect—and that no one else is either. That is what it is like to be human. Everyone carries some level of pain and suffering with them. Take the time to treat everyone with care, as you would like to be treated. And treat yourself the same way.

Day Three: Forgiveness

I recall Maya Angelou referring to forgiveness as a gift. "Forgive everybody," she instructed. I understand what she meant when she said it was "one of the greatest gifts you can give yourself." Forgiveness, to me, is how we shine light on the darkness. Give yourself this gift on day three. You must forgive yourself. Allow yourself some breathing room. When you forgive, you release yourself from the anger, hurt, blame, folly, criticism, and stupidity that you carry inside. You genuinely feel lighter after letting go. I work at it, and I have felt the lightness that comes from forgiving others, and especially forgiving myself, so I stay at it. I'm chipping away at the massive wall of blame and hurt that has surrounded me. It liberates me. It allows light in. It eliminates the darkness.

Day Four: Gratitude

On the fourth day, take some time to reflect on all you have as opposed to everything you don't, beginning with the marvel of our existence and the opportunity it affords us to experience what I consider to be the best part of being human—giving and receiving love and affection. Betty White is my role model. I've never seen or met anyone more thankful than my former Hot in Cleveland co-star. She starts each day with gratitude for everything she has been through and excitement for the day, which includes her two favourite indulgences, vodka and hot dogs. The woman practically shines. Take a cue from her. Thank God for your health. Be thankful for having enough to eat and, hopefully, some to share. Be thankful for having a place to live that keeps you warm and safe. Be thankful for the opportunity to share your experiences with others. Consider the last time you laughed and loved. You're now grinning. Everything else is a bonus.

Day Five: Kindness

Remember the way you smiled the day before? On the fifth day, do something that puts that same kind of smile on someone else.

Day Six: Joy

On the sixth day, step outside—literally outside—and outside of yourself. Experience other people, the world, the universe. You will have to figure out the specifics for yourself, but that is what I try to do. I try to turn off everything in my head that says, Me, me, me; and if I truly make the effort and am lucky and alert, I will inevitably feel joy.

Day Seven: Love

If you make the effort on the previous six days, the seventh will be effortless. You will have added the weight of a paper clip and feel like you lost a mini microwave. Without having to do anything, love will find you. Love enters an open heart, and when you do this for six days, love will enter. And there's a danger in this. Once in a while, you will feel hurt. But as I am learning, love is there more often than not.

Disclaimer

I make no promises. I offer no before and after pictures as evidence that this diet will put you in a smaller dress size. But it will put you in a better frame of mind. It does me. While I am far from perfect and my days can suck just like anybody else's, and I still hate sitting in front of my magnifying mirror when I pluck my eyebrows, I am learning that by intentionally practising these values, one per day, I am usually able to treat myself better and love others more and open myself up to the possibility of experiencing joy immediately. At this moment. At this age. In this body. That's what I want to feel.

CHAPTER 9

BUBBA AND BEAU

SPRING 2020

I'm more worried about losing Ed than I was about losing my parents. That sounds bad, I know. My folks were wonderful. But my relationship with Ed is unique. The thought of never being able to share a thought with him that only he would understand, or ask him a question that only he would know the answer to, or trade smiles across a room as we watch our son appear onstage in front of an audience that wants to see him just... well... that kind of loss scares me indescribably.

When Van Halen was on tour in 2015, I assumed Ed would recover from cancer. For a decade and a half, he had battled the condition in various portions of his tongue and throat. He received the greatest medical treatment available. Of course, he could have helped himself earlier by quitting smoking and drinking. Cancer is not something you spit at. You don't make fun of the Big C. You don't act as if you can outrun it. Ed, on the other hand, eventually got over his denial and rage and got his sh*t together. He looked after himself, and it showed. He felt and looked wonderful. Then he was in a motorcycle accident and discovered that he had cancer that had grown throughout his body like a greedy developer gone wild. Despite this, we stayed optimistic, trusted the medicines, and clung to promising checkups. He was joyful, caring, and appreciative despite being sober in every aspect.

He is still that way. Hopeful.

The other day, we texted. He, like everyone else, was looking for a new TV show and asked if I had any suggestions. Everyone seems to be talking about Netflix, Amazon Prime, and HBO these days. This pandemic has rendered all of us housebound. I never imagined my parents getting old or unwell until they did. My mother was slowed in her forties by rheumatoid arthritis, which worsened over time, yet both of my parents lived into the age of sixty-five. They relocated to Las Vegas after my father retired from General Motors after 32 years of service. "No state income tax," he stated. My father was a Fox News devotee who influenced me more than any book, TV show, movie, documentary, or person I heard speak could. I believe he was aware of this and took pride in having a strong, independent daughter who could care for herself.

However, we normally avoided discussing politics and highly personal issues, preferring to keep conversations light and superficial. There were far too many traps. My father was a good provider and a loving parent, but he was not a true husband, which left scars on all of us. When we gathered around the table, football was a much safer topic to discuss. My brothers all played, my father aided the coaches, and my mother and I became Sunday and Monday night die-hards, as familiar with sweeps, draws, and sacks as we were with the latest Bloomingdale's catalogue. That hasn't changed. My parents relocated to Scottsdale, Arizona, in 2004. Patrick, my youngest brother, who resided in Scottsdale with his wife, Stacy, saw that they were slowing down. He stated that it would be easier if my parents were closer to them because he and Stacy were the ones who checked on them the most frequently. We assisted my parents in finding a magnificent home, and they spent around 10 years enjoying the dry desert air before a series of mild heart attacks and related health difficulties sapped my father's energy.

Then, one day, he drove my mother to a doctor's appointment, and the nurse at the front desk, who knew my parents well, grew concerned when she saw him. He stated that he was fatigued. She rushed him into an examination room, where it was discovered that he was experiencing a heart attack at the time. He was saved by the nurse. We were sad, afraid, and realistic as he recovered. This was the inevitable next stage of adulthood, when you became the guardian of your own parents. My brothers and I talked about it and asked each other the same questions that so many of our peers and individuals our age seemed to be asking: Can Mom and Dad take care of themselves? What should we do? How can we assist?

It's one of those things you never consider. It's not like when you were younger and spent a lot of time imagining what it would be like to get your driver's licence, live in your own apartment, have sex, get married, and have a child. Then your parents get sick, slip, or forget, and suddenly their care consumes all of your thoughts. Patrick and Stacy took the lead, and I gave whatever assistance was required. My parents were lucky to have the means to provide decent options for themselves. We discovered a lovely one-bedroom apartment in a cosy assisted-living facility. Going through their possessions, which had gathered over sixty-one years of marriage, was understandably upsetting because we had to pick what to save, donate, and toss; and practically every item had some form of narrative or personal link to it. It was simple to find furniture. It either fit or didn't fit in their new abode. If it didn't fit, the four of us discussed who wanted it and what to do if no one wanted it. Appliances, electronics, and photographs were all handled in the same way. The task prompted reflections not only on what accumulates over a lifetime and what is required to build a life and raise a family, but also on how we children broke away from our parents and formed our own lives. Is it true that I was just eighteen when I bought my first home? And I was just twenty-one when I got married?

My father was extremely organised and kept everything in precisely labelled bins. We discovered deeds and contracts for our previous residences. Art work and reports from school were kept in folders. There was an old baby book for my brother, Mark, with congratulatory cards from relatives and friends pinned in the front. Of course, the book stopped abruptly and was, I assumed, stored aside until we found it again. That wasn't the only delicate family issue we discovered. We discovered a handwritten letter from my father's half brother, whom we had never seen, while sorting through boxes and albums of photos and paperwork. We knew Nazzareno had come to America, met my grandmother, and had three children—my father and his two sisters, Norma and Adeline—but we had no idea he had abandoned another family back home in Italy. It was a genuine "holy shit" find.

"Dear Andrew," began the letter. "This is your brother Ernesto writing to you. I believe you are familiar with our past. When I was three years old, our father left me in Italy and went to live in America. He wrote to me, and I know you're my genuine brother. I have a huge desire to meet you directly."

We wondered if they'd ever met and came to the conclusion that they hadn't. However, who knew? We decided not to mention it to Dad. What was the point if not to know—and now we did. But I noticed a parallel between Nazzareno and my father. Both held secrets, some of which had affected their families. They were like old-fashioned Italian restaurants: white tablecloths, stiff cloth napkins, the smell of garlic rising from the kitchen, a menu with classic antipasto, fried calamari, spaghetti marinara, fettuccine alfredo, and a back area where nobody knew about. I wasn't immediately ready to forgive my father, but I had a greater understanding of him. He didn't have the best teacher when it came to becoming a husband.

One of our requirements for the move was that their cat, Beau, accompany them to the assisted-living facility. They were devoted to him. My parents only had one of their two cats at the time. Bubba, their second cat, had gone missing six months before. My cell phone called as we were on our way to have one more look at the new flat before signing the lease. A woman on the other end of the line asked whether I had lost a cat.

"What do you mean?" I said, believing Beau had gotten out of the home because we had been in and out so much.

"It's a white cat with an orange tail and blue eyes," explained the woman. "But he looks like he's been out on the streets for a while."

I placed the phone down and scratched my head, telling her to hold for a second. I had to think about it. Then it struck me.

"You didn't just happen to find Bubba, did you?" I inquired.

"Um, I don't know if it's Bubba," she admitted. "I discovered a clearly abandoned cat."

"Where did you find him?" I inquired.

She informed me. She became enraged when I mentioned that it was less than a mile from my parents' house.

"This poor cat," she lamented. "We assumed he had been abandoned... because, you know, a lot of people do." Unfortunately, people no longer wish to care for their cats and abandon them in feral colonies."

"No, no, no, you don't understand," I said, adding that we were distraught when we couldn't find Bubba despite posting leaflets all over town. Bubba had been living behind the local grocery shop, where employees and the owner of the dry cleaners next door fed him but couldn't catch him for six months. They had him scanned and called the number on file, which was my cell phone, once they had him. Bubba was my father's cat, and he was overjoyed to have him back. Beau was as well. They all moved into an assisted-living facility. My parents were in bed when I arrived a few days later, and Bubba and Beau were cuddled up on the bed with them, as if they'd never been apart. My parents were content with their routine at the assisted-living facility. My father was downstairs one day, being Mr.

Helpful as was his wont, when he noticed a woman who appeared to be about to fall. He dashed over to her side and caught her just as she fell. He broke her fall, but she landed on top of him, breaking his hip. He never recovered from that point onward. I can't help but think of the old adage: "It won't kill you to be nice." Except in his case, it did. He died on December 7, 2016, just six weeks after the accident. I have a photo of Bubba sitting on the bed with my father after he took his last breath. Dad was all set to depart. His kitty companion, albeit sad, was nonetheless bringing solace. I mourned and grieved with the rest of my family until the routine of talking to and checking in on my parents became primarily centred on my mother. Sadness arrived in waves. The space between the waves was filled with worry for my mother. She was devastated when my father died. Whatever his flaws as a spouse had been in the past, she had accepted them long ago, and he had done the same, becoming a devoted carer as her rheumatoid arthritis curtailed her activities and filled her days with suffering.

I'm not sure why cruelty and compassion frequently go hand in hand, but they do. Is it possible that they are two sides of the same coin? It makes no sense. My mother had a difficult life. She was born in Jersey and was just nine years old when her mother died. Her stepmother was terrible, and I'm fairly certain she was sexually molested as a teenager. She never stated such words clearly, but she dropped hints and made it plain she was eager to leave her residence. She ran into my father as she exited a movie theatre in Claymont, Delaware, one snowy winter night. He showed up in his car as she waited for a bus and offered her a lift home. She refused. He drove away, but then turned around and begged her to accept a ride rather than stand in the chilly weather. They married five months later. I wish this had been the end of her difficulties. Unfortunately, it did not. My father's family treated her terribly throughout the first few years of their marriage since she wasn't Italian or Catholic. My brother Mark died, and my father's family held that tragedy against her as well. Devastated, she coped by attempting to be a better mother and wife. The gods remained unkind. My father had an affair with her. She was diagnosed with rheumatoid arthritis in her forties and lived with agony for the rest of her life. She was never given a respite. What was the purpose?

I've always wondered the same thing about Mark. What was the point of his life, or any life, if it was going to expire so quickly? My poor mother. She had a hysterectomy when I was about eight or nine years old. She took me to a doctor's visit one day. I guess no one was able to observe me. In the front seat of the automobile, I sat next to her. Every time she hit a pothole, she grimaced in pain and turned to apologise to me. For what purpose? Why did she feel the need to apologise when she was the one in pain? Years later, when her arthritis began to cripple her, she did the same thing. She did this even as she was failing later in life. It didn't make any sense. I should have grabbed her and apologised for all of the pain she'd undergone and was still dealing with throughout her life. I did tell her how wonderful she was and how much I loved and appreciated her, and how I knew all the good fortune and abundance I had in my life would not have been possible if she hadn't given birth to me, driven carpool, sat on sets, and put her own desires and ambitions on hold to be a great mom.

But I couldn't have a meaningful, personal conversation with her. Not about my brother Mark's death. Not about my father's infidelity. It has nothing to do with arthritis. Not the way her arthritis eventually compelled her to give up painting. Not about how it reduced her life to weekly doctor's appointments and regular medication, eventually leaving her immobile. I never claimed I understood or was sorry for what she had gone through. I never said I understood, and if you need to cry, cry. She only came near once, when I was in my late twenties. We were bickering over something, and she was on the verge of disclosing her grief, whatever it was at the time, when I stopped her.

"Don't," I advised. "Don't even think about going there."

"Why don't you want to be close to me?" she questioned in a way that I will never forget. "Why can't we be friends?"

It wasn't that I didn't want to be close to him, or that we weren't. It was because I didn't want to witness her anguish. I was terrified, terrified of what would happen if those wounds were uncovered. I didn't see how being more open and honest with each other would have benefitted either of us. We wouldn't have had to lug around so much crap. When I'm overwhelmed by feelings and emotions, I isolate and shut down until I shrug and accept the negativity or suffering as a part of me. "Well, that's just me." I learned from the greatest. This is the aspect of my work that I am seeking to change and let go of. I don't have to keep what's in my heart hidden. I don't have to beat myself up about things that happened a long time ago. I don't have to suffer as a result of ingrained behaviour. And I don't have to constantly feel like there's something wrong with me that I need to work on.

I am fine.
I am good.
I am bad.
I am broken.
I am perfect the way I am.
I am human.
I can do something my mother wasn't able to do. I can love myself. As I am. At this age. Right now.
It's enough already.

My mother lived for three years after my father died. Given how much suffering she was frequently in, I questioned why she survived rather than him. Her back was gone, she'd had two knee procedures, and she was always looking for the ideal combination of medications to help her. It was almost as though God kept her around to torment her more. She was not a Buddhist who thought life was all about suffering. She was intelligent, gorgeous, sensitive, witty, and extremely gifted. I was absolutely perplexed by her circumstances. What was the purpose?

She appeared to unwind when Dad left. When I went to see her, I made sure Bubba and Beau were fed and clean, and that their litter box was empty, and we sat and spoke about the cats as if they were part of our family, which they were. We watched ancient films. Summertime, a Katharine Hepburn film, was a favourite of my mother's. It happened in Venice, and we discussed returning even though she wasn't strong enough to travel to California, let alone fly across the ocean. On Sundays, when I visited, we would watch football together. She wore her favourite player, the renowned wide receiver Larry Fitzgerald, in her red number 11 Arizona Cardinals jersey, while I arrived in my number 9 Saints jersey with BREES written on the back. She hosted a Super Bowl party at the assisted-living facility one year.

I used to always surprise her with a large bag of Cheetos, which she adored. I did as well. They triggered recollections in me. I used to pack a small bag of Cheetos, a sandwich, and a can of Pepsi for lunch every day while I was in high school. So my mother and I reminisced—two girls who had spent the most of their life dieting in the same way that Thelma and Louise ran from the law were eating Cheetos and licking their fingers without guilt or shame. What became clear to me was how eating was our bridge to communicating and bonding in ways we had never done before. That's how I discovered my father's family had been cruel to her after my parents' marriage, and how they eventually warmed up to her after she spent years standing alongside them in my Aunt Adeline's basement kitchen, listening to them talk about the family and the old country while making pasta. She was essentially an English-Irish girl who had to learn Italian.

Even though she held the scars of those traumatic experiences, she was able to laugh about them sixty years later. She was victorious. She outlived them all. That is the ultimate goal. The only way to find out what happens next is to wake up in the morning. It also allows you to have the final say if you so desire. Only the living have the ability to write or rewrite history. But my mother didn't give a damn about revising anything, and I realised that the three years she spent without my father allowed her to **let** go of the responsibilities, slights, hurt, and critiques of the past **and** simply exhale. She, like me, could say, "Enough already."

I certainly hope so. My mother died **peacefully** in her sleep on June 18, 2019, the day before her 65th **wedding** anniversary. She had collapsed the previous year and had **been** basically bedridden since January. Her body was gradually **disintegrating**. Patrick and Stacy called to inform her that she was **closing** down. I was perplexed, almost in denial of what I already **knew** was unavoidable, and I inquired as to how they knew. "You **know**," Patrick admitted. I was going to wake up and go to start **on** season seven of Kids Baking Championship when I got the call **that** she had left. I was pleased that she was no longer in pain and that her **ordeal** was done. She had been in a lot of agony by the end. I still w**ent** t**o** work since you don't go to work if you don't show up, and Ed **called** me when I was in the makeup chair. Wolfie had told him **about** my mother, and we had a heartbreaking conversation.

He then texted me a photo of himself **with** my mother. He's wrapped his arm around her. My mother is s**miling** at the camera, and Ed is staring at her tenderly. He seemed **more** distressed than I was, and I realised why. Ed was aware that his **cancer** had spread, and he was contemplating the gravity of the news **and** the battle ahead of him. I still didn't know about his predic**ament** at the time—either because he wasn't ready to tell me or because **he** believed the timing wasn't right. But my mother's death **impacted** both of us hard. It communicated to both of us that time **does** not wait for anyone. Don't squander it. I'm reminded of this every **time** I come into my sunroom, or "catio," and see Bubba and Beau **cuddled** up together on the chair or in the cat tree.

CHAPTER 10

BLESSINGS

JULY 2020

It's summer—the middle of July—and nothing is happening. Covid has shut everything down. Everyone is confused, scared, depressed, and anxious. Ordinarily, I would be travelling a couple of times a month to food festivals, speaking engagements, New York City, and maybe taking a vacation. But I have not gone anywhere or done much of anything.

I miss travelling. The more I am not in Italy, the more I want to be there. I also want to go to London. I just want to go. Somewhere. In a few weeks, we are taping the new season of Kids Baking Championship. The Food Network has found a hotel an hour south of me in Palos Verdes where we can create our own bubble and shoot the episodes with everyone getting tested beforehand and wearing masks throughout production. I am looking forward to getting back together with my pal, master baker Duff Goldman, the crew, and a new batch of talented kid bakers.

Actually, I am eager to be around other people again. I am hungry for conversation, laughter, stories, and cute pictures of children and pets. It has only been about a month or so since Wolfie and Andraia decided that it was safe to come inside the house when visiting me. The three of us were tired of waving and yelling through the windows. Our temperatures were normal, our hands were washed, rewashed, and wrinkled, and we were not going anyplace other than the grocery store. So I told them to come in. "The door is open."

"Hi, Ma!" Wolfie said.

My arms were already wide open and ready to grab him. We hugged. I didn't let go. It had been way too long. My eyes filled with tears. I could feel my soul inflate inside me. Never underestimate the power of a hug. Since then, Wolfie has been coming over with more frequency, and those hugs are more important than ever. Between Covid and Ed, the backdrop has been so gloomy. The hugs reignite my sense of hope. My spirit lightens after each one. Forget those stickers on the back of cars that say MY CHILD IS AN HONOUR STUDENT. I want one that says MY KID HUGS ME. It is a blessing—and like most blessings, it is delivered in a small package that is so ordinary looking it's easy to overlook or take it for granted.

You have to pay attention or else you are going to miss the joys in life. That has been my problem. I have not been paying attention. It has been seven months since I went on the Today show and announced that I wanted to stop letting my concerns about my weight cast a negative shadow over everything in my life and to experience joy instead. As I was right then. In my body. At my age. I didn't want to always think I had to fix something about myself. It was enough already. As I told Angie Johnsey, the mind coach the Today show introduced to me, I sensed that I would find I wasn't all that broken if only I could get myself to see more of the good.

Either that or everybody is kind of broken, and being kind of broken is actually normal and okay. Angie worked with me on recognizing the voices in my head that spoke to me, especially the one that always said I needed to lose ten pounds before I could even begin to think of myself as being on the right track. Then Covid hit. The world went full stop.

I turned sixty.

Ed's battle with cancer took a turn none of us had wanted to imagine.

I didn't see my son in person for months.

I didn't see anyone for months.

Life became extremely slow. Clothes were kept hidden in favour of sweatpants and pjs. Every day was either a Tuesday, a Wednesday, a Friday, or a Saturday. It didn't make a difference. The cats, on the other hand, purred and sprawled out in the sunlight. The squirrels were chased by the dog. The flowers began to bloom. The trees began to bear fruit. The scent of orange blossoms and jasmine filled the air. I relished the sun's warmth. I enjoyed the peace and quiet. And in the silence that surrounded me, I accomplished what had eluded me for so long. I started counting my blessings.

I didn't even have to put in any effort. One day, I was reminded of the exquisite simplicity of a bologna sandwich, similar to the kind I used to have for lunch in elementary school. Oscar Mayer bologna atop two slices of Wonder Bread with mayonnaise. The taste, the soft white bread, the gooey, buttery sweetness of the mayo, and the suppleness of the bologna slices all appealed to me.

What do you think? I was grinning from ear to ear as I remembered those sandwiches.

It was a blessing that I had parents, a family, and a mother who prepared my lunch, as well as that I wasn't hungry.

Later, I remembered my beautiful cat Dexter, who died of cancer when he was thirteen years old. He was by my side during the darkest years of my life. It was a blessing. After a few days, I found myself picturing myself on a helicopter with Ed, flying into Devore, California, for the US Festival. It was May 1983, and Van Halen was headlining the heavy metal portion of a three-day desert festival organised by Apple cofounder Steve Wozniak. We swept over the vast wave of people below us as the pilot focused in on his landing point, several hundred thousand metal fans dancing to Mötley Crüe, Ozzy Osbourne, and other bands while eagerly awaited Ed and company. Ed was shaking his head in amazement and chuckling from nerves and incredulity. They performed for two hours that night. Ed looked lovely in overalls that complemented his Frankenstein guitar. David Lee Roth was infuriatingly clever. The entire encounter felt like a crazy dream, the craziest, wildest, best dream imaginable.

Thirty-seven years later, I was in my backyard, staring out at the wide-open view across the valley and picturing that image, when I burst out laughing. I shook my head in the same manner Ed had done in the helicopter. Disbelief. Is that what happened? That truly did happen. Oh my goodness. It was a blessing. So here I am today, in sweatpants and a T-shirt, with no idea how much I weigh and no plans to get on a scale this week or next. Yes, I could lose ten pounds, and I wouldn't mind losing twenty, but my viewpoint is unaffected. I don't need to look good in a bikini. Physically, my current objective is to be healthy enough when I'm eighty to climb the stairs to my bedroom without assistance or heavy breathing. Obviously, I am a realist rather than an overachiever. In the meantime, I'll keep counting...

My family has been a blessing. Getting a position on One Day at a Time when I was so young was thanks to Norman Lear, the greatest producer in television history, whose track record could have made him a terrifying tyrant. He was, nevertheless, kind, gentle, nurturing, lovely, and loving. I'm collaborating with Bonnie Franklin, Pat Harrington, and Mackenzie Phillips. Each of them taught me in their own unique way. Bonnie, who was quite talented, taught me the nuances of acting. Mac, although being only six months my senior, had matured far faster and was a paragon of strength, wisdom, and resiliency. Pat also taught me the value of time. It was a blessing to meet Ed. It was also a blessing not to have social media at the time. Otherwise, I would have probably blogged some idiotic things or been videotaped acting like an idiot, and I would still be paying for it today. Wolfie. The gift of being hot in Cleveland developed into five years of sheer delight. Do you hear what I'm saying? I mentioned "joy." Not only that. I dubbed it "pure joy."

That it was. The script arrived around the end of 2009. I'd never heard of TV Land, the cable station that was creating it, which had previously aired reruns and movies. However, I was informed that they were now creating their own unique content. I read the script, which is about three Los Angeles-based showbiz ladies whose plane to Paris makes an emergency landing in Cleveland, Ohio, where they decide to remain and rent a house with an eccentric elderly caregiver who lives a full and busy life despite her age. The script was fantastic. The show was said to be talking to Jane Leeves and Wendie Malick, while Betty White had already been cast as the caretaker. I didn't know which part they wanted me to play, but when I heard the names of the other women, I responded, "Okay, I'm in." I had no idea the producers were giving the same story to Jane and Wendie and getting the same reaction. Everyone registered. We did our first table read in February 2010, and we were on the air in June.

The five years I worked on that series were the best years of my life at work. Jane had been one of my closest friends since Faith Ford first introduced us when Wolfie was a baby. Wendie quickly became a close friend as well. And Betty White was just as people imagine her to be—funny and quick-witted, with an outlook that inspired me every day I was in her company; the woman actually shined. She was definitely a beacon of brightness. And our guest stars—Carl Reiner, Mary Tyler Moore, Tim Conway, Cloris Leachman, Carol Burnett, Joan Rivers, and so many more—were a who's who of entertainers who made me a fangirl every week.

All blessings—and far too many more to list.

I won two Emmys a month before my mother died. Mom was unable to watch since the 2019 Daytime Emmy Awards were streamed live on Facebook rather than on conventional television, which was too much for her at her age and health. After that, I called her to tell her the wonderful news.

"I am so happy for you," she exclaimed. "You thoroughly deserve it."

Did I? Was she correct? I won a Golden Globe for my work on One Day at a Time in 1981. I won again in 1982 for Best Supporting Actress in a Series. My mother was my date the first year. Ed joined me the following year. Both times, I was taken aback. Nothing else comes to mind. An Internet search of those events simply serves to remind me that life is a succession of hairstyles that become less humiliating as you get older, especially if you grew up in the 1980s. A life lesson is hidden somewhere in those blow-dried curls.

The Globes were always in a bookcase. I put them in the library after Ed and I renovated our house. They then followed me to my current residence, where they sat on a shelf in my office at the back of the house. They made excellent bookends. I occasionally saw them. I ignored them the majority of the time.

But I've always wanted an Emmy. It was something that suggested your work was acknowledged and your talent was respected by your peers, and I was always looking for something that would provide the validation I couldn't feel on my own. When I was watching award programs, I imagined what I would say if my name was called. I didn't want to be the person who reads names off a list. It turned out that I didn't need to be concerned. Despite countless shows and hundreds of films, I managed to avoid being nominated. The pressure wasn't only wrong. It was never turned on. I had a fantastic time, but I was able to convince myself that I wasn't very good. Then, after giving up acting for an apron, I was nominated for two Emmys.

I was completely taken aback. Even though I had shot nearly one hundred episodes, an equal number of short video tutorials, and grown more comfortable in the kitchen, I read and reread the online notification and text messages that came in and kept asking myself, Really? It was incredible, and no one was more astounded than I was. I still had far too many days when I felt like an imposter. It wasn't that I was acting, that I lacked the necessary talents, or that I wasn't working my tail off every day to constantly learn and develop. No, I was afraid that some online troll would call me out for pretending to be a TV chef, and even though there was nothing deceptive about my work in the kitchen, that one criticism, even if it was the lone negative comment out of a thousand compliments, always triggered a rash of self-doubt and irritated me for days.

It was the old childhood gremlin, the feeling that nothing was sufficient. Feeling... undeserving. I wish I had the strength to ignore the remarks on my social media accounts. I know better, yet I can't stop myself from staring at them. They are generally upbeat, kind, and considerate. They make me happy and make me feel like I've made hundreds of pals throughout the years. The nasty aspect is that I seek out the Negative Nellies because they validate my worst fears about myself. They've seen the genuine me. Except that the real me was in the ninth season of my cooking program, grateful for the nomination, and maybe, just maybe, deserved. I told myself to relax. I knew I wasn't going to win the Emmys, so I was able to relax and enjoy getting dressed up and going to the party on the big day. My main concern was whether my pants would fit. Does this sound familiar to anyone? Lori, my show's stylist, had brought over a black tuxedo jacket and pants for me to try on, change, and return earlier in the week. However, things change. But today was my lucky day. They are appropriate.

I've known Lisa Ashley, the makeup artist, and Kimmie Urgel, the hair stylist, since our Hot in Cleveland days, and we've become friends, so hair and makeup were a snap. That left one more worry: hoping that my shoes wouldn't be too unpleasant and cause my feet to throb in the middle of the play. Did I have these concerns when I was twenty-three? My husband, Tom, and I drove to the theatre with executive producers Jack Grossbart and Marc Schwartz, who also happened to be my long-term manager. I was sitting next to Giada, who was nominated in the same categories as me, and I thought to myself, I'll watch her walk up and accept the award, and I'll be fine with it because she deserves it. She's incredible. I was pushed to the aisle just before the show started, where I sat next to Jeopardy! Alex Trebek, who had previously appeared on Hot in Cleveland, was a really witty and compassionate man.

Rachael Ray, a friend and early inspiration of mine, went onstage to read the nominees and announce the winner of my first category, Outstanding Culinary Program. I was thinking how great it would be if I won my first Emmy and received it from Rachael, since I adored her and knew she would be overjoyed. I'd even been a correspondent for her show. Then, during the small gap before she read the winner's name, I noticed her excitement and realised it was my turn, and I erupted into tears.

I was taken aback. I made it up the steps and onto the stage without tripping, despite my tears. Then, despite years of planning what I would say if I ever won an Emmy, I realised I had nothing prepared. I didn't bother because I was certain I wouldn't win. What did come out of me was real disbelief, which I simply articulated in two words: "Holy [fill in the blank]." I received my second Emmy of the night for Best Culinary Host a few moments later. I invited all of my producers to join me onstage, and then I thanked everyone I could think of. Nobody does anything by themselves, and my huge realisation, in retrospect, is that appreciation is the stairway to joy.

After my coffee and Advil kicked in, I went out for drinks that night and called my mom and brothers the next morning. I did something rare for me: I allowed myself to bask in the affirmation granted by those sculptures, which I placed on the kitchen table, ready to repel an attack by the feared opponent known as imposter syndrome. As prizes are wont to do, I let them boost my confidence in myself, and eventually I stopped beating myself up and let belief and pride seep into my self-esteem. All of my hard work, study, and experience were paying off. I relocated the Emmys to the dining-room table a few weeks later so I could see them as soon as I stepped through the front door. Good day, Best Culinary Host. Hello, and welcome back. Excellent Culinary Program

Almost a year later, I relocated the gleaming statues to the top of a cabinet near the entryway, where they are less conspicuous. I can see them, and they can see me, but other people don't need to wear sunglasses every time they walk in. After a few more months, I dig out my two Golden Globes from hiding and place them next to the Emmys on a whim. Suddenly, there is a mob on top of the cabinet, a meeting of old and new friends. Meet my Golden Globes, Emmys. Meet my Emmys, Golden Globes. I am proud of them and everything they stand for, and that is fine with me. Even better is the way I perceive myself. I hear my mother say, "You deserve it." I believe her sometimes, maybe even most of the time now. And let me tell you, that is a blessing.

CHAPTER 11

MY MOTHER'S RECIPE BOX

JULY 2020

Despite the fact that it's summer and I should be creating a light, warm-weather meal for dinner, I'm craving lasagna. On the counter is a recipe card labelled MOM'S LASAGNA, although I don't really need it. I drew it from the recipe box out of habit. I've done this dance enough times that I know the steps by memory. I start with the onion and garlic, then add the ground beef, sweet Italian sausage, and hot Italian sausage, seasoning them all before moving on to the besciamella, which is a touch I added to my mother's recipe years ago, much to her chagrin.

The kitchen fills with the strong garlicky perfume that I recall from our favourite restaurant in Florence, and my eyelids close reflexively as I appreciate the flavour in the air. I remark to myself after a spoonful of self-satisfied chuckle, "Hey, I should have my own cooking show." The lasagna noodles will come next. But I'm cut off when the phone rings. It's a robocall asking whether I want to extend the warranty on my automobile. Really? Now? I don't know anyone who hasn't received this call at least forty times. We don't need our car warranties to be extended. Attention robocallers: Please stop selling warranties, informing me that my Social Security card has been stolen, informing me that someone has charged $700 on my Amazon card, which I do not have, and so on.

Enough is enough. Still, the timing of the call suggests that it could have been my mother calling from another dimension to warn me that it's not lasagna unless I use ricotta cheese. This was a point she made to me on a regular basis and with good-natured glee, as if we were discussing two sides of a spending bill on CNN.

save that there was nothing to argue about, save personal preference. There are only two flaws in lasagna. One question: Do you use ricotta? My mum agreed. I say there's no need. Second, who gets the crispy corners? This, according to my mother, is the greatest part of any lasagna. Before the meal arrives at the table, it is frequently the basis of family feuds and covert picking. Am I correct? When I hear of folks who dislike this aspect, I am always astounded. Are they also among those who avoid the cream-cheese frosting on carrot cake because they don't like it? I'll never comprehend that move.

Can we agree that carrot cake, no matter how good it is, is nothing more than a vehicle for cream-cheese icing, which is reminiscent of the sweet taste of your first kiss from your first crush? To return to the original point, lasagna has much more than four crispy corners. The flavours combine and merge extensively during baking in a well-made lasagna, but there are still little areas where the bite packs an explosive burst of oregano or basil or a chunk of wine-soaked sausage with a nugget of melted Parmesan stuck like a salty barnacle. It's a tongue dance down the Spanish Steps that makes your entire body stand and applaud, from the hair on your head to the tip of your toes.

This is why the dish has remained basically unchanged since the Middle Ages. It's the reason I became interested in cooking. I was eighteen, living alone for the first time, and coming out of my Chef Boyardee phase—that brief moment when everything I cooked came from a can or the freezer. I had a craving for lasagna. I adored my mother's lasagna almost as much as I adored anything else. My mother handed me the hand-written letter that is now on my kitchen counter one afternoon as I drove home.

My mother's lasagna had its origins in my grandmother's kitchen, which meant it was truly Italian, as the ancient Greeks are claimed to have introduced the first recipe to Rome in the second century. That is, my mother's recipe has been tried and proven for years. Except for Thanksgiving and Christmas, it was her go-to for any special event.

"What should I know about making it?" I inquired.

"It's easy," she said. "Come over and watch me make it the next time I make it."

"Watch me" was the important phrase in her offer. Lasagna is one of those dishes that can be made from a recipe card, although my mother never followed it exactly. My Nonnie didn't either. The foundations are the same, but there's always a pinch of this, a smidgeon of that, and maybe a smidgeon of something else. You can take the freeway or the blue highways and back roads and arrive at the same location, but the experience along the route determines how you feel about the journey.

I recall doing it for the first time on my own in my tiny little abode. I pulled it out of the oven, nibbled on a corner, and when I eventually got a full-size slice, I thought, Whoa, that's wonderful. I can prepare meals.

It eventually became my go-to. Even when The Silver Palate Cookbook's chicken Marbella became the go-to dish for impressing relatives and friends, I still depended on my mother's lasagna. It was made for Ed and Wolfie. It was done for my parents. It was made for my brothers. When all of us met at the beach house for important occasions, I joyfully proclaimed its arrival fresh from the oven. I told its narrative in the first episode of Valerie's Home Cooking's ninth season, "Honouring Nonnie."

I modified my mother's recipe somewhere along the way. Instead of ricotta, I used Parmesan and a creamy béchamel, a white sauce created from a roux and milk, like she did. My variation is known as lasagna alla besciamella. My mother referred to her lasagna as "the proper way to make lasagna."

After my first cookbook was published, she called me to say that she found a mistake.

"Where?" I asked.

"The lasagna," she said.

"What's wrong with it?" I asked, concerned about a misprint.

"There's no ricotta," she said.

"Oh, we're going to do this?" I replied.

"I'm sure it's still delicious," she said. "It's just not right."

I laughed. "Okay, you English-Irish woman."

The only thing that rivals the charred corners about lasagna is getting the leftovers out of the fridge the next day, which is what I do. The unwinnable debate follows: Is leftover lasagna better hot or cold?

For those who prefer it warm, I recommend cutting a piece and baking it at 350 degrees for about twenty minutes; avoid a rapid microwave hit. The wait will be worthwhile. I slice a thin piece, arrange it on a dish, and eat it cold. It reminds me of a multilayer cake, savoury without the sweetness, and it is satisfying in a manner that tells me my craving for lasagna the day before was more about nourishing my soul than my stomach—just like it is now.

Ed has been causing me concern. I've also been thinking about Wolfie, how close he is to Ed, and how his love is like a string he keeps tying in ever tighter and smaller knots in a valiant and unwavering effort to keep a much larger ship from drifting away in a strong current. My son is very private. Divorce erected an impenetrable barrier. The majority of our interactions are on a need-to-know basis. Cancer has not altered this. I sometimes have to coax information from him. I'm worried that he got the best of Ed and the worst of me. Yet, every now and then, we stare at one other with familiarity, terror, and quick understanding, no words necessary. I adore my son so much that it hurts. The way I believe he feels about his father and me.

People in therapy talk about needing a toolbox, with different tools for different scenarios. My mother's recipe box is now mine. When

I'm stuck for ideas, I reach for the recipe box. I also travel there when I need to communicate with people who came before me and are still hovering close in that invisible region. When I brought it home after we transferred my parents to assisted care, it provided reminders and helped me reset in ways I didn't expect. The recipes are written in my mother's lovely script. Some are as sharp and new as they were the day she wrote them. Others are aged and soiled, and include not only recipes but also stories; they are three-by-five platters on which memories are brought to the table and delectably recalled.

As in the lasagna. I could hear myself phoning her and asking how to make it the first time I brought out the card yesterday. Today's topic is a different one: How do you deal with it? Where is the appropriate card? In the category of appetisers? What about meat and poultry? Salads? Dessert? My mother and I were never very close, to the point where I would seek her advice during difficult times. Perhaps I underestimated her—and ourselves. I used to have a lot of questions when I was younger. What ingredients do you use in your beef loaf? What exactly was in Nonnie's red sauce? What method do you use to make your cheesecake? She was continually telling me.

Let us now hear what she has to say. I go through my toolbox and pick out a card. Rings of onion. The card appears to have spent a lot of time next to the stove, bent and discoloured by what I think are streaks of grease and oil. Except I don't recall her preparing onion rings on a regular basis. The following card I pull is named NEW ORLEANS RED BEANS & RICE. After my mother and my father relocated to Louisiana, she became obsessed with New Orleans-style cuisine, and although I wasn't living at home at the time, I recall her serving these with almost everything when I visited.

I play another card. It's almost like a game now. As though I were dealing tarot cards. Bread. Huh. Plain white bread. I read the directions aloud. "Two cups of lukewarm water; one package or a cake of yeast."

I pause to reflect. I have several large jars of yeast. How much does a package cost? Approximately two and a quarter teaspoons.

"Two teaspoons sugar, two teaspoons salt, and three cups of flour." Melt five tablespoons of margarine in a saucepan. Mix in three more cups of flour and knead for ten minutes. Place in a greased mixing bowl."

The recipe comes to an end there. I turn to the back of the card, hoping to locate the remaining steps, but it's blank. I just see a smudge, a fingerprint—my mother's.

"How many rises, Mom?" I say. "Should I make a loaf?" Or should I roll the dough into small rolls? What's the story? What happened to the rest? It's unusual for you to leave something incomplete."

Then I understood. She is speaking to me as clearly as she did before. It is referred to as the staff of life in the Bible. At the Last Supper, Jesus distributed unleavened bread as a metaphor of his broken body. It satisfies the physical body's needs. It also nourishes the soul. It is a divine gift. It has the ability to sustain life. It is possible to share it.

"Take this, and eat..."

I don't think it was by chance that I brought up a bread recipe. Or that the final steps were left up to me to figure out.

The recipes in that little box tell a more interesting tale than I realised, from the early days of my parents' marriage, when my mother was learning to cook and striving for acceptance, to my first eight years in Delaware and my parents' moves to Michigan, Los Angeles, Oklahoma, and Shreveport. Almost all of my family supper memories are from when we lived in Delaware. I remember eating at the kitchen table or, on special occasions, in the dining room, where my mother had painted a whole wall with a lovely mural of the Italian coast from the perspective of people sitting on a balcony.

I'm not sure how she managed to plan and paint such a monumental piece while caring for four little children and making three meals a day for a family of six. She also sewed all of my outfits as well as those for my Barbie dolls. We moved to Michigan when I was eight years old, then to Los Angeles in 1971, and by fifteen, I was spending most of my time at the studio working on One Day at a Time. A year or two later, someone on set introduced me to café au lait, and I thought my taste had improved dramatically. At eighteen, I was living on my own and enjoyed eating at the Moustache Café, a chic French bistro on Melrose Avenue. I chose quiche, which struck me as the pinnacle of elegance. I taught myself how to prepare it and proudly served it to my parents.

Quiche is what it's called.

Meet my folks, Quiche.

My mother then called one day to tell me that she had discovered a recipe for Famous Amos cookies.

"The actual cookies?" I inquired.

"Yes. "It's the famous Amos chocolate chip cookies," she explained.

"I need to make a copy of that recipe," I added.

For fun, I rummage through the recipe box's dessert area and find the card: FAMOUS AMOS COOKIES. I grabbed an armful of cookbooks the day I brought home my mother's recipe box, several dating back to the early 1950s and one from 1947. Aside from a slew of dishware, cutlery, and pots and pans that I opted to donate, I took a long, hard look at her pot holders: two gigantic gloves with black burn marks on the palm sides. The cloth was paper thin; she had worn them for as long as I could remember, until they were no longer usable. They went in the trash. Remembering this helps to alleviate my concerns about Ed and Wolfie. Recipes can be distributed. It's a continuing discussion. I was going to have to do everything alone, including handling hot plates, heavy lifting, and labour. However, I appreciated and embraced any and all assistance along the road.

Which is ironic. For so long, I was afraid to ask for help. In anything. I was under the false presumptions of youth and ignorance that I shouldn't admit I didn't know how to do something. It turns out that asking for help is easy. Years ago, I asked Ed to teach me how to play a particular Patty Griffin song that I liked. I sang a bit of it for him.

"Oh yeah, that's easy," he said, grabbing a guitar—one of the many that always seemed to be within his arm's reach—and strumming the song as if he had played it a hundred times. Then he handed me the guitar and showed me the first and second chords and the up and down rhythm of the strum as he slowly guided my hand.

"Okay, now you try it," he said.

I began the song in fine form but stopped abruptly just a few words in and turned to Ed with a look of helplessness.

"How do you do that chord again?"

"Oh come on, it's easy," he said.

"Easy for you."

I can still picture where the two of us were sitting that night.

CHAPTER 12

LEARNING HOW TO LISTEN

SUMMER 2020

Wolfie phones late in the afternoon to say he'd like to come over to the house and play with Bubba. He arrives with his girlfriend, Andraia, whom I admire, but not as much as Henry, a giant, fluffy, white cat who is head over heels in love with her. He claims they've both had a hard, tiring day at their respective jobs and want to unwind away from their devices.

"Are you going to stay for dinner?" I inquire.

"No, we're just going to hang out," he clarifies.

"I'll make something," I promise.

"You don't have to," he points out.

We're eating dinner two hours later. When Wolfie indicated they were going to hang out, I knew they were staying. "We're just going to hang out" implied they had no plans for the evening. "Hang out" is code for "the rest of the day and night is open." Of course, nothing is open and no one is going anywhere these days, but I could tell by Wolfie's tone that he wanted to go home, where his mother would prepare dinner and he could cuddle with his cats.

I cooked tuna melts for dinner because I didn't have anything else in the fridge. I combined the tuna with a couple of hard-boiled eggs, a great and undervalued combo in my opinion, and topped it with a few slices of provolone, though pepper jack would have been my first choice if I had any on hand.

The sandwiches have been consumed. As we eat, I catch up with Andraia, who is smart, interesting, and intriguing to talk to, even though I barely comprehend half of what she says about her work. In addition to modelling, she works as a software developer for one of the major computer businesses. I admire her for being a young woman who leads with her intelligence. She majored in computer science in college after catching the programming bug as a young girl. She tells me that when she was eleven years old, she wanted to construct a Backstreet Boys website and study the page code.

"You just read the page code and understood it?" I inquire.

"Yes," she confirms.

"I love it," I declare. "I'm not even sure where to look for the page code."

Wolfie is quiet and pleased to listen to Andraia and me talk until I mention going to our beach cottage for the weekend. He leans forward, smiling impishly, and suggests he might go on eBay and hunt for replacements for the computer games he lost in the "flood." The flood occurred about fifteen years ago. A leak in my bathroom leaked into the playroom just beneath it, destroying Wolfie's computer game collection. They had to be removed. His lasting distress and laughter make me laugh.

"It's not funny," he adds flatly. "Those were the sacred games."

I have raised eyebrows at him. "Sacred?"

"I used to have a Sega Genesis." There was also a Saturn console, which was unusual. And a Sega Pico, which was a pretty fantastic kids' learning centre. And even more. "Everything was ruined."

"Sorry," I respond, cringing as I recall that scenario.

"How did the flood get so bad?" Andraia wonders.

"I didn't hear the drip," I explained.

Now it's Wolfie's turn to raise his eyebrows at me. "For the next three years?"

I will not confirm or deny anything.

My issue isn't whether or not I can hear. It's about what I hear and don't hear. For the majority of my life, I had only heard the criticism I levelled at myself when I glanced in the mirror. When I stepped on the scale, I verified it. The details changed, as did the number on the scale, but the message remained consistent: you need to be fixed. Which I interpreted to mean "you need to lose ten pounds."

I was telling myself things like, "Go see Mom and Dad," "Follow your passion," and "Check in on Ed," and I was lucky to have heard those things. But You need to shed 10 pounds and drown out everything else. And the truth was that those 10 pounds, or whatever number came up that day, symbolised all the other concerns and insecurities I wasn't addressing.

Here's how it works. When you carry a heavy bag of emotions around and don't deal with them, you become that hefty sack. Similarly, if all you tell yourself is that you are big and need to lose weight, you will never hear others say that you are charming, humorous, brilliant, generous, and kind—all of the qualities that make a person truly beautiful. It was a present. I simply couldn't hear it. That you've-got-to-lose-ten-pounds voice rendered everything else inaudible. Not only couldn't I hear myself think, but I couldn't hear anything or anyone else, even all the people who had approached me throughout the years and complimented me. Imagine receiving a blessing and being unable to hear it. Missing Mozart, for example. Or a bottle of champagne popping and the sound of a newborn laughing.

Hearing the negative was easier and more credible for me. Even when the facts and the entire world screamed otherwise, the whispers in my head verified everything I told myself when I missed the number on the scale. So much was lost to me. I was jolted awake from a deep slumber one night shortly after Ed and I married by noise—music being played repeatedly outside the bedroom door. I was irritated. I didn't even notice the catchy tune. Instead, a voice in my thoughts asked, "Does he have to do that now?" When do I have to go to work early in the morning?

I tried rolling over and closing my eyes more tightly. I placed the cushion on top of my head. I could still hear the music—ba-ba-ba-ba-ba. Finally, I stood up, crossed the dark room, and opened the door to see my husband seated on the floor in front of his small synthesiser, a knot of elbows and knees and long brown hair hovering over a keyboard. He gave me a sheepish grin as he gazed up at me. Edgar, our cat, was curled up in his lap. Edgar also looked up at me. They were both aware that I was enraged.

"Sorry," Ed apologised.

"You have to do that here?" I inquired. "Right outside the bedroom door?"

He shook his head. He acted as if he couldn't help himself.

"Please stop," I pleaded as gently as I could. "I implore you to halt. I need to get up at five o'clock in the morning."

As I closed the door and returned to bed, I heard Ed remark, "Love you," and the music resumed for a minute or so before he got up from the floor and worked the rest of the night in his music room down the hall. Ed didn't listen to me, which was a good thing. That tune has now become known as "Jump." It was Van Halen's first and only number one single, appearing on the band's 1984 album. We've been laughing about it for years. When I first heard Wolfie's music, I began to learn how to listen. Wolfie was on tour with Van Halen in the summer of 2015. This was his final and third tour with the band. I met up with them back East, eager to see him, and one afternoon Wolfie asked if I wanted to hear something he was working on. He was unconcerned about it. He didn't say anything about writing music. He didn't describe it as his own original music. He explained that it was "some stuff I'm working on."

He was shy, cautious, and guarded, as is typical of him, but as a Wolfie-speak specialist, I understood that, in addition to rehearsals, video games, and his girlfriend, this "stuff" had to be significant to him.

"They're rough, not even fully developed demos," he warned as we got into the tour bus's rear seat.

I couldn't say anything after his first song, "Epiphany." Halfway through the second song, "Resolve," I was struggling to keep it together and failing miserably. Because that's where I was stuffing all the emotion, the back of my throat felt swollen, achy, and ready to burst.

"One more?" he inquired.

I agreed by nodding. The dam ruptured at that point. "Distance," the third song, was a quiet, sombre ballad that began with a basic percussion and a guitar pluck. I heard Wolfie's voice after the song had been playing for a few seconds. He was singing. I turned to face him. He was waiting for my reaction.

"I don't have the words just yet," he admitted.

"I still almost hear them," I replied, closing my eyes and allowing the music to wash over me. "It's almost like I can hear the words."

Then I did it. The chorus began, and I could hear Wolfie singing.

I hugged Wolfie and listened to the rest of the song with him in my arms, without trying to wipe the tears from my eyes. We had no idea Ed would become so ill at the time. We had waited three years to learn that the cancer had spread. But Wolfie, who had been touring and recording with Van Halen since 2007, had already been through a lot with his father, and whether he knew it or not, he was preparing himself for the next inevitable stage, and he was doing a much better job than I was. I couldn't be more pleased.

I literally dragged Ed away from wherever he was going later that day when I spotted him backstage at the arena and asked if he had heard Wolfie's song.

"Yeah," he agreed.

"Can you believe it?" I wondered.

His eyes glowed like they always did when he talked about Wolfie, and he brushed away a tear.

"I know," he admitted. "He's amazing."

Even in Wolfie's early, raw, unfinished state, I heard so much of what we had talked about over the years, what Wolfie and his dad had talked about, what the three of us had discussed when we got together, and what all of us individually had thought or were thinking but were too afraid to say. Wolfie's talent and emotions, his sensitivity and passion, and... his love, I heard.

"How do you do it?" I was curious.

"Like Dad," he explained. "I listen to music."

When Wolfie was a kid, I'd take him on the Van Halen tour so he could spend time with his father, and Ed would bring him onstage for a father-son duet. I believe that was Ed's favourite part of the play, and Wolfie enjoyed it as well—the novelty, the crowd, and, most importantly, making his father happy. I hoped he wouldn't pursue a career in music. It was and still is a difficult business. People are extremely critical. And with his surname, everything was going to be considerably more difficult. Every note he played was compared to his father's music. As he grew older, I accepted the idea that he didn't have a choice. Wolfie possessed the gift of hearing music in his thoughts, the air, or wherever those ideas came from, in addition to an abundance of natural aptitude. Ed allowed him to not only listen to it, but also to follow it. He encouraged him to write and play. Ed was aware of the impact music might have on people by conveying feelings such as happiness, despair, joy, enthusiasm, and the thrill of being alive in the moment. He understood it had the potential to improve people's lives. It had altered his life.

Nothing impacted Ed's life more than touring with Wolfie on three Van Halen tours. Until he heard Wolfie's own song, that is. I felt the same way after listening. But Wolfie wouldn't let me hear his music demos again until 2018. They had lyrics this time. They were still being manufactured, but they were more polished and put together. Wolfie authored all of the songs, including the music and lyrics, and he performed every instrument. I was so struck by what he was able to say in those songs—thoughts about love, depression, and regret—that I sat in astonishment and stared at him.

Later that night, I texted him, praising everything he'd done as a musician, sharing my concerns about him going into music, but finally explaining that it was his gifts as a songwriter that had helped me understand the depths of his artistry and, more importantly, that those songs had given me insight into him as a young man, and I loved what I heard.

"Thank you for letting me listen," I said. "I'm in love with you."

Wolfie was planning to release his album and go on tour in 2018, but when Ed found that his cancer had advanced, he put everything on hold to spend time with his father. He utilised the time to experiment and fine-tune his tunes, and every now and then I heard an improved version of one of them. He remarked once that Ed's favourite song was "Think It Over." I was envious. I wanted a copy of the songs so I could listen to them sufficiently to select a favourite.

I didn't need to pick a favourite. However, as a proud mother, I required a CD of those tunes. They're all of them.

"Fine," he replied. "The next time you come over to my house, I'll upload them onto your phone."

The same day Ed arrived, I went over to Wolfie's house and we all shared the spinach and crab dip I had left over from The Kelly Clarkson Show. I was the first to arrive and handed Wolfie my phone while I made the dip and set the crackers and crudités on a platter. I couldn't wait to get his songs. He couldn't wait for me to sit down and listen to his music. But he suddenly changed his mind about putting them on my phone.

"Can you just listen to them right here?" he said. "You can come over whenever you want."

"It's just for me," I explained. "I've been asking for it for months."

"But—"

"I promise I won't play them for anyone." I began to cry.

"Oh, my God, Mom," he exclaimed. "I didn't think you'd be like this."

He hugged me as he moved across the kitchen.

"I'll give you the songs," he assured her.

Wolfie had finished downloading all of the music and was showing me where I could locate them on my phone when Ed opened the front door. He was also playing his music through his home speakers at my request. The music was loud, as our family prefers their rock and roll. Ed cocked his head sideways and listened. His eyes glowed with pride. His grin had grown even brighter. I raised my head from my phone, matching his grin.

"Hiya," I introduced myself. "He's just downloaded his songs onto my phone."

"Nice," he remarked with a nod of approval.

"Hey, what's that?" he asked, pointing to the bowl of spinach and crab dip and crackers on the table.

"It's delicious," I declared.

Months after Ed and I talked in George Lopez's car on Thanksgiving, I remembered an Italian proverb that claimed wisdom comes from listening and repentance comes from speaking. That explains how I felt during that chat. When Ed expressed his connection and closeness to me, as well as his love, adding that he hoped it didn't seem strange or awkward, it had a greater impact on me than I realised at the time. I felt good about what I was able to tell him, and when we walked back inside, I assumed that was the end of the conversation, thoughts shared, everything good. But I kept thinking about it and continued to do so. It allowed me to witness how our twenty-year marriage blossomed into a friendship, then into a different kind of love. I was already aware of this. However, hearing that from Ed felt nice at the time and even better as time passed. Ed was in the hospital the next time I saw him. It was January 2020, and he was recovering from a back operation. When I entered his room, he was still in his underwear, brushing his teeth. He appeared to be in wonderful health for someone who had cancer in his lungs, brain, and wherever else it had spread. A thick white bandage wrapped across the area on his back where he underwent surgery a few days before. He was bobbing his head to Wolfie's music, which was blasting from a few of Ed's speakers at an unusually loud volume for a hospital.

"Pretty good," I admitted.

"It's fucking amazing," he exclaimed.

Life has altered six months later. We are confined to our dwellings, see only people in our pods, and must wear masks when venturing outside. According to my sources, we may film the Kids Baking

Championship later this summer. Normally, this would result in panic, followed by a diet, followed by anxiety. However, my personal work, as well as my work with Angie, is assisting me in managing the voices in my head that are constantly pressuring me to lose ten pounds, be better, and fix myself.

I hear those voices, acknowledge them, and try to figure out what they want before putting them in the Trash Room, the Past Room, or another storage container. I hear alternative voices in their place, more positive, gentler, and loving voices. It has an impact. Worries and fears about being on camera are put to rest, and I am able to focus on how much fun it will be to hang out with my friend Duff and laugh with all of the amazing kid bakers on the show.

The same goes for my own child. When Wolfie tells me about Ed, I'm not filtering it through my own mental noise. Instead, I am present for him and better able to comprehend that he communicates in code, telling me what he believes I need to know about Ed as well as what he believes I need to know as his mother. The two are not synonymous. It's remarkable what I can hear when my mind is clear. It's the same as driving with a clean windshield.

I only wish I could have done this sooner. I recall my conflicts with my mother and that one fight at the beach house years ago. When she questioned why I didn't want to communicate and be closer, I believe she meant why wouldn't you open up to me and allow me to open up to you. I couldn't—not with her around. Simply put, there was too much muck. Just because she was ready to reveal herself didn't imply I was. I didn't have that skill set at the time.

I wish it had been different. I observe other moms and daughters who have close relationships and wonder how my life and my mother's life would have been different if we had been that way as well. In so many ways, we were similar. She ate her feelings. She was constantly on a diet. She didn't fully mature until much later in life. It makes me sad for what could have been, but maybe that's how it was meant to be.

Ed and I had to wait until Thanksgiving to communicate and hear what was actually going on in each other's hearts. I wish we had done it ten years ago. It's a brilliant, shining moment in the midst of a terribly strange and sad year. But Ed and I exchange texts. Even though going to visit this damn Covid makes me nervous, I swear to stop by if I ever go anywhere other than the grocery store.

Surprisingly, I've been hearing the intro to Van Halen's "Women in Love" in my head. Though Ed composed it before we met, I've loved it since the first time I heard it. I usually asked him to play it backstage at gigs while he was tuning his guitars and warming up his fingers. "Please play it," was all I had to say, and he understood precisely what I wanted to hear. He'd sneak it into one of his solos and look to me on the side of the stage with a naughty sparkle in his eyes to see whether I was paying attention.

I'm motivated to create more positive memories by listening to wonderful music. To that aim, my child has the best advice. I ask Wolfie about crafting the words to his songs one day. I am impressed by the sensitivity and breadth of his subjects. I struggled to articulate my emotions when I was his age. Getting a grip on them was difficult. Even at my advanced age, I am continuously learning. Wolfie reveals that melody comes before words, but when composing, he comes up with mouth shapes—"words and phrases that feel good in my mouth," he says.

"Instead of trying to shoehorn a bunch of words into a song because I've written them down in my notebook, I listen for words that sound good and feel good."

"You listen for a feel?" I inquire.

"You can hear when something sounds right."

I understand. That is how I finally learnt to listen.

CHAPTER 13

I DON'T KNOW HOW MUCH LONGER WE HAVE

OCTOBER 2020

There is something in Wolfie's voice one day. I hear it whether it's a change in his tone, a catch in his throat, or just my mother's intuition.

I didn't say anything at first. I don't want to, yet I'm at a loss for words.

I have a habit of blurting out whatever is on my mind, sometimes for the better, sometimes for the worse, and this is one of those instances when I don't want to blow it. As a result, I tend to bite my tongue.

Wolfie contacts me from outside Ed's room at Saint John's Hospital in Santa Monica a little time later.

"I don't know how much longer we have," he admits.

My brother Patrick had stated the same thing about my mother to me. She lived for another six months after he rang the alarm.

This is a unique circumstance. I'm aware of it. Wolfie's voice tells me so. He wouldn't be telling me this if it weren't true—and it's probably worse than he's letting on.

"Okay, I'll be there," I say.

Though Covid has complicated matters and robbed us of valuable time together, being there for each other in some manner has been the focus of our life for much of the year. Wolfie had left Ed's hospital room a few weeks before, looking for me. The look in his eyes when I spotted him in the hall said it all. I stretched out impulsively, and he collapsed into my arms. My six-foot-tall son. I wrapped my arms around him as tightly as I could. I'm not sure where maternal strength comes from, but I had a lot of it and wanted to give it to him.

"I'm sorry you're going through this," I apologised. "I'm sorry your father is having to go through this. I'm sorry for everyone."

Wolfie nodded, his head buried on my shoulder.

"You've been so strong for so long," I commented. "You're allowed to be weak. You no longer need to be strong."

I make a commitment to myself to go to the hospital every day. I feel unprepared, as if this has come as a surprise to me. I recall Ed casually saying two years ago at Wolfie's rehearsal that he had recently been diagnosed with brain cancer. He was very casual about it, as if he was telling me about his new automobile. I later learned he had stage IV lung cancer, though I don't recall Ed or Wolfie telling me the cancer had spread there as well. If they did, it appears improbable that it was registered. I can't think I'd hear "stage IV" and not be terrified.

But I've been seeing Ed battle cancer for the past two decades. I always believed him when he stated he was going to beat it. He swatted it away with the latest medications and treatments every time it appeared. Ed outperforms everyone. He is pulled over for drunk driving, yet he is not arrested or even ticketed. Why? He's Eddie Van Halen, after all. His talent has made life a magical carpet ride.

Not that he didn't face difficulties. His childhood was difficult. Because of their parents' mixed heritage, Ed and Alex were subjected to racist remarks and mocked as half-breeds when they relocated from Indonesia to the Netherlands. They were severely poor after relocating to Pasadena. They shared a home with several other families. His mother was a maid, and his father was a janitor. Ed was crying as he told me about their false Christmas presents—boxes that were wrapped but empty, so that when guests came over, they would assume the Van Halens were just like any other family.

He was a kind old soul with a great sensitive heart. It killed him because he had caused harm to others. He was anguished by the knowledge that he had previously damaged me and disappointed his son. In the acknowledgements of my 2008 book Losing It, I wrote to Ed, "You're a good man, believe it." When you do, you will be liberated." I didn't want him to feel bad about things that happened in the past. I had already forgiven him. I wished he would forgive himself.

When he finally got clean five years ago, he was able to let go and discover that he was the decent, kindhearted man I had described, and I believe he truly enjoyed taking a step back, inhaling, and knowing that he didn't have anything else to prove to anyone, especially himself. He was liberated.

But it's far from finished. Ed had recovered from his back surgery by mid-March and was scheduled to return to Germany for additional cancer therapy. My brother Patrick was accompanying him. When Covid struck, flights to Europe were cancelled, and Ed, like the rest of us, took refuge at home. Throughout the summer, we texted and FaceTimed. He spent much of his time on his sofa watching TV between doctor appointments. I couldn't see how his health was deteriorating or how quickly it was deteriorating, and Ed didn't say anything to me when we spoke.

I regret not asking more questions.

I wish I had phoned more frequently.

I wish I could have simply dropped by his place with dinner. What are you up to? Do you mind if I join you on the couch for a while?

I didn't think that was my concern.

The dreaded Covid. It was our Berlin Wall, The Hunger Games' electrified fence, and Lost's sonar barrier. It pulled us away from the simple pleasures that make life rich and meaningful—human contact, touch, and kindness. It reminded me of being on a diet. We craved these things more as we were deprived of them.

Neither Ed nor I ever considered getting back together. But I knew he had my back, and he knew I had his.

I texted him, "Thinking of you," accompanied with a cat-hugging GIF.

There was no reaction.

After a few days...

"Morning, just checking in to see how you're feeling," I reply back.

"Terrible," he says. "I've got a lump on my neck." Cancer is a pain."

"I'm truly sorry."

"How are things going for you?"

"I think of you every single day."

"Thanks. This stinks."

August 29, I textEd: "40 years ago you were playing Shreveport, LA, and my life changed forever. I hope you're doing well and feeling well."

"40 years!!! That's insane!! Changed mine too!!! Love you Val, hope you're good."

Ed had a mild stroke in September. He was already in the hospital, so he received quick medical attention, which was the lone bright point in an otherwise bleak sky.

We weren't ready to give up the fight against cancer, but it was proving to be a tenacious, unyielding, and callous foe. I began to let go of the assumption that there would always be a tomorrow, even though I didn't want to admit it and kept these dreadful feelings to myself. I'll see you tomorrow. I'll call you tomorrow. Let's meet up next weekend. We should get together for dinner.

Instead, I concentrated all of my efforts on the now. I didn't want to spend any time. I was texting Wolfie if I wasn't with Ed.

Our interactions had been reduced to a few crucial words.

Good.

Awake.

Comfortable.

Sleeping.

Ed is having difficulty speaking one day. It's afternoon, and Wolfie and I are with him, along with the rest of the group. Ed has attempted to communicate multiple times after the stroke, but we have been unable to comprehend him. After numerous attempts, Wolfie finally removes Ed's oxygen mask and says, "What do you need?"

Ed smiles, his gaze concentrated on Wolfie's, and says with great clarity, "Pizza, please."

Laughter floods the room. Ed's eyes sparkle. I'm not sure if he's made a joke or is hungry and wants another slice of pepperoni for the road. He enjoys pizza. In any case, knowing he is still among us fills my heart.

Ed's doctor enters his hospital room just after Wolfie notifies me that time is running out. Looking straight at Ed while simultaneously connecting with Wolfie, he adds there's not much else they can do for Ed. They can, however, continue to fight if Ed so desires. Without missing a beat, Ed says, "Let's keep fighting."

Wolfie and I will be at Ed's hospital room every day for the next week and a half. We sit on either side of him, telling stories, making sure he's comfortable, and telling him we love him. Wolfie is holding one hand, while I am holding the other. We try not to leave him alone, so if one or both of us are absent, Ed's brother fills in. Janie is also present. Ed is aware that he is surrounded by the individuals who love him the most.

Wolfie and Ed swap earbuds while listening to Wolfie's music. They've been listening to music together since Wolfie was in diapers and Ed sat him on his lap while he played the piano or guitar. Ed's face lights up when he hears "Think It Over," his favourite song. It is the album's most pop-sounding song, with lyrics about regret and looking back on past mistakes. Ed, on the other hand, has clearly thought things through, made his peace, and all that matters to him is being with his son at this point. They hold hands and cherish every second they have with each other while they listen, just as they used to, just like always.

I spent Friday night sitting on Ed's bed. It's just the two of us for a bit. I take his hand in mine. I brush his brow. I look him in the eyes and smile.

"Maybe next time, right?" I say.

We're both crying.

"Maybe next time we'll get it right."

In this situation, we are just like any other family. Time does not stop so much as it ceases to exist. We are aware that the sand in the hourglass is running low, but we do not look. Our primary concern is the here and now. People talk about being present in the moment. Nothing puts you in the moment and makes you appreciate what it is to live like losing someone you care about. As I sit there, it's all I can think about. This is what is important. Love.

Everything else fades away in the end. Love is all that remains. Only love is genuine. Slowly, the end approaches. We spend hours with him on Saturday, taking turns holding his hands, stroking his arm, gazing into his eyes, and saying the only thing that matters, "I love you." We make certain that he is at ease. My heart is breaking, and

I'm not sure how that can be when it's so full of love. Perhaps it is overflowing and about to burst.

Ed keeps staring off into the distance at night. He notices someone and appears to hear them as well. His expression is light, serene, curious, and alert. I notice him smiling. Someone is clearly welcoming him, assuring him that he will be well, and offering him comfort, and I want to know who is there. But another part of me refuses to accept that this is happening. We're still fighting and hoping. Ed then informs us that he is quite weary. Wolfie and I get up and gather our belongings. I kissEd on the cheek.

"Sleep well," I advise.

"I'm so tired, I just can't sleep," he complains.

"Try," I suggest. "I adore you." I'll see you later."

"I love you, too," he admits.

He tells Wolfie the same thing. "I'm in love with you."

Ed had another stroke later that night, after we'd all departed. When Alex arrives in the morning, he is unable to awaken Ed. He phones Wolfie and tells him, "I've been trying to wake your dad for a half hour and haven't been able to." Wolfie dials my number, and we rush to the hospital. We arrive in his room just as Ed is being carried back in after having a brain scan. His doctor follows us and displays the scans. We don't need an explanation to observe the damage. It's a disaster.

"Listen, I know we said we were going to fight, and Ed wanted to fight, but I don't know if we can ever get him awake again," the doctor says. "What we can do is make him very comfortable."

That's exactly what they do. He'll be there till Monday. Wolfie phones me on Tuesday morning to tell me that Ed's breathing has changed and that I need to hurry to the hospital very away.

I dash through the city, breaking speed restrictions and cutting the thirty-minute commute in half. But I can't find a parking spot at the hospital. A classic Los Angeles issue. I'm on the phone with Wolfie, who is pleading with me to hurry up. I saw a man walking towards his automobile. Score! However, he is pursued by a heavily pregnant wife and a toddler who refuses to cooperate as they attempt to get him in his car seat. I've been there, but why can't they speed up?

"It's taking them forever," I say to Wolfie.

I finally park into the spot and dash into the hospital after five minutes (it felt like an hour). I don't check to see if I need to feed a metre or if I'm in a ten-minute zone. I don't mind. Allow them to ticket me or tow my automobile. I stop at the lobby desk and go through the Covid procedure I'm all too familiar with. My temperature is taken, I am given a fresh mask, and I must wait for a pass.

"Please hurry," I request. "He's dying."

The hospital staff understands my panic and apologises because they've seen individuals go through this before. I dash across the foyer and onto the first elevator that comes to life. I activate the fourth-floor button. A woman steps in at the last second and pushes two. My patience has never been more tested. The extra few seconds seem interminable. Why couldn't she just go up the stairs? I believe.

Why didn't I just dash up the stairs? I tell myself it's a lesson. Right? It's a learning experience. Wolfie is holding Ed's hand when I eventually go to his room. Malcolm, Alex's son, is at the foot of the bed. I pull up a chair and take Ed's other hand in mine. Aric, Alex's other kid, comes at some point. Janie feels the same way. Ed has changed in my opinion. He appears to have waited for all of us. We tell him how much we adore him.

"I love you" are the last words Ed speaks to Wolfie and me, and they are the last words we say to him before he ceases breathing. Soon later, a doctor arrives, examines his pulse, and announces the time of death. It's just past ten o'clock in the morning.

Nobody moves or speaks once the doctor leaves the room. The weight of the moment renders us all immovable, frozen in time. Janie leaves after around twenty minutes because she wants to be with her family. The rest of us remain. Until the door opens, I lose track of time. A chaplain enters and asks if we want some rosaries. She reappears a few moments later, passes out the rosaries, and blesses them. More time has passed. None of us wants to leave Ed. Not right now. Never, ever. We are one big family. We share tales about Ed and the Van Halens. Alex recalls Indonesian phrases that used to make them chuckle when they were kids. We tell each other anecdotes about Ed's sense of humour. Suddenly, we're all laughing. It's strange. I never imagined being in that hospital room hours after Ed died and laughing as hard or as much as I did, but that is exactly what happened. We laugh—and it's so much better than sobbing, which we do quite frequently.

Someone eventually asks whether anyone wants pizza.

"I think Ed would want that," Alex suggests.

Everyone is in agreement. Alex smiles as he pulls out his phone and gets three huge pepperoni pizzas from a nearby pizza joint. It appears strange, right, and Ed.

I'm feeling numb. I wake up in the middle of the night, sick to my stomach, and rush to the bathroom. I feel like I'm rehashing the entire year. I haven't puked in decades. I go back to bed and sleep till the wee hours of the morning. Late that afternoon, I head to Wolfie's place and prepare a boyhood favourite for him and Andraia: franks and beans. Food for relaxation.

Patrick approaches to give assistance. We went through many family photo albums that I brought over after dinner. My father put them together many years ago. We trade recollections and anecdotes as if we were playing cards, attempting to outdo one other with more tears and more laughs. What happened to Ed? Why is he overlooking this? Perhaps he isn't. He can be felt in the room. Wolfie is inspired by it.

"Ma, I want to finish 'Distance' and release it for Dad," he says.

"That's perfect," I responded before breaking down in tears. I can't help myself. My eyes welled up with tears. "It's really perfect."

A few days later, Patrick and I are back at Wolfie's house, watching old family Super 8 films that he and our friend Dave had turned to DVDs a while back. When Wolfie was around three years old, one of the three of us—Ed, Wolfie, and I—was at the beach. It's sheer delight. We keep watching it over and over. Faith Ford, I believe, was the one who took the video, and as we were rewatching it, Faith called from her home in Louisiana to express her sympathies.

When I tell Wolfie who is on the phone, he exclaims, "Are you kidding me?"

"I know, right?" I say.

Now I'm certain Ed is with us.

I'm not sure how we got from watching these movies and looking at family photos to discussing how they could be assembled and made into the video for "Distance," but we all agree that there is no better way to convey Wolfie's beautiful song. Ed's music touched so many people and was and continues to be such an essential part of their lives that it feels appropriate to share this very personal element of his and our life through Wolfie's song.

We discuss it and agree that it can serve as a reminder that love is the best part of us and should be treasured.

As we view these videos, I know my heart is filled with love.

It's adrift on a sea of tears.

It is completely full. And it's still afloat. My thoughts keep returning to Ed in the hospital room, as though I'm trying to understand and digest what happened despite the fact that I know what happened. But I have a new realisation. The love we shared lasted with me while I sat there holding Ed's hand, grieving as he left his physical body, and it still does and always will. Wolfie decides to release "Distance" as well as include it on his album. "Now it just feels right," he says. We cry when he plays it for us.

CHAPTER 14

SCROLLING HAPPY

NOVEMBER 2020

This morning I awoke drowsy. Groggy means I'm out of bed, my eyes are open, but I'm half-asleep. I'm still unable to see clearly. I need to walk with my arms outstretched and hands out, feeling the wall and gripping the bannister for dear life, as if I'm lost in the dark. Even the first cup of coffee does not immediately clear the fog.

This is not the same as being grumpy. When I switch on TV news while reading the newspaper, I sink in a puddle of disillusionment and rage. What's so difficult about assisting those in need?

We have a slew of well-paid individuals with free lifetime health insurance who are producing more problems than they are solving. Most of them are old men who obfuscate the facts and transform history into fiction in order to defend the interests of businesses and their own personal power. What does it mean to make America great?

Greatness, in my opinion, recognizes the helpless and the destitute. Greatness strives for equity and opposes injustice. Greatness extends a helping hand and a welcoming heart. Greatness motivates actions of courage, optimism, and humanity.

But don't get me started on it. Not while I'm still groggy.

This concludes my morning.

Coffee.

Cats.

Walk the dog.

Crossword.

Silence.

A lengthy, relaxing stretch in the sun.

That's much better.

In the aftermath of Ed's death, I'm navigating my way through the fog of grief. "Distance" by Wolfie debuts at number one. Emotional triggers are amplified. I give myself room and time. Words run through my mind like freeway signs: exhale. grace. Patience. Breathe. Small steps. Laughter. Gratitude.

On the day "Distance" is released, Wolfie is interviewed by Howard Stern, who is one of the finest, if not the best, interviewers in the media as long as you aren't the one being interrogated, as I discovered years ago when he concentrated on my rear end until I shouted at him to stop.

He is respectful, compassionate, and supportive of Wolfie. My favourite part of their talk is when Wolfie shows Howard the first instrument his father got him and verifies Ed was the worst guitar teacher in the world. Ed would show Wolfie a riff and say, "Do this," and Wolfie, a beginner at the time, would look at his father and say, "I can't do that." You look like Eddie Van Halen."

As I listened to the interview, I recallEd sitting Wolfie on his lap and playing the piano, his fingers dancing across the keys to his little son's joy. Our library had a piano. Ed had a lot of fun playing there.

He congratulated me one day for designing a room with superb acoustics. I was taken aback. I did? Okay... nice.

As time passes, the tears fade into a more bearable and familiar flow. The holidays are difficult, especially when I want to contact or text Ed and realise I can't, despite the fact that his number is still in my phone, along with years of texts. I'm working on recalibrating this shift; Ed is gone but yet very much present. He is all over the web. Along with David. Along with Sammy. Along with Wolfie. His breathtaking solos. His underappreciated piano skills. That music will live on in perpetuity. Ed isn't going anywhere.

He appears in my mind as well. Our nuptials. His automobiles. The insanity. The way we cause each other harm. The anniversaries. There were the phone calls. The excursions. The way he turned to me and grinned from the side of the stage thirty-five years ago because we were a couple, but more recently because we were thrilled by our child. The man who dazzled audiences with his musical prowess was dazzled by his son. And I enjoyed it. The conflict between past and present is unending and unresolved.

Love always triumphs.

That is why it hurts so much.

Grief is one of those things that you have to wade into and expect to cry your way out of.

Talking and remembering are beneficial. Pictures serve as stepping stones. Nighttime isn't as frightening as it was when you were used to hearing the phone ring and hearing that familiar voice say hello or hey, what's up.

I'm doing precisely what Angie Johnsey advised about a year ago: acknowledging the voice in my head, addressing it, and putting it in its proper place.

The sadness does not fade as much as I improve at dealing with it. I recognize it, communicate with it, and employ it. Grief seems to hit me hardest when my tank is empty, but instead of allowing it to knock me down, I use it to fill it back up. Someone should design a T-shirt that reads, EMOTIONS ARE THE WORST THING TO AVOID.

I want to cook not to eat but to create, connect, and share with people. One day, I make my four-cheese crab mac 'n' cheese, which includes two cups of cheddar cheese, a cup of Gruyère, a cup of fontina, shredded Parmesan, and a pound of jumbo lump crabmeat topped with panko crumbs and scallions. I'm craving my kale Caesar salad with garlicky panko crunch in a few weeks. I pronounce it a punch to the taste buds after finishing the dressing with fresh garlic and anchovies. "Yes!" I exclaim, alone in the kitchen.

Later, I published another video of myself cooking this salad on Instagram. Faith Ford describes it as a "yum explosion" in the comments. It is, and her reaction makes me feel lighter and more optimistic. This is more rewarding than my previous method of dealing with my feelings. I'm in the kitchen right now. The lights are turned on, and there is no sneaking, no passing judgement, and no defining myself as terrible. Hoda, where are you? Savannah? Carson? I wish they were here to witness me laughing instead of grieving for once. And wanting more.

Please, more.

Inspired, I go on social media to see what else makes others happy. What are people's recipes for happiness? This is some of what I discovered.

My household

A beautiful day

Laughing

Hearing my child's voice (he's 47 and in the military, but he's still my baby)

Hearing the doctor tell me that my husband survived surgery "It's harmless!"

My first appointment is with my therapist. I haven't seen her since before Ed died, which was undoubtedly a mistake, and we're having a productive session. She assists me in peeling back the layers until our roles appear to be flipped and I am describing the issue to her. I'm stuck, and I'm not doing anything to get out of it. Then I outline the steps I must take to get unstuck. Isolate yourself. Snacks should be avoided. Instead of three glasses of wine, have one. Step outside. Move my buttocks. And are in line with my interests. If I'm confined in a dark room, Joy won't be able to find me.

I'm at the chiropractor's office in a few days. Because this is the first time I've seen her, I enter cautiously, wearing a mask, and she takes my temperature and assures me that she, too, is healthy and following protocols. I'm soon laying facedown on her cushioned massage table, crying buckets of tears into my mask as she lovingly works on my legs and body, saying something to herself about my life energy.

"Do you find that most of your patients cry the first time they see you?" I ask.

She might have reacted, but what she tells me a few minutes later erases all memory of it. While poking and pressing my back, knees, and neck, she comments that my top rib is out of place and is causing my neck and shoulder pain, which strikes me as strange but nowhere near as strange as when she states we aren't alone.

"Huh?" I ask, speaking directly into the face rest hole where my chin and mouth fit.

"I can feel your mom in the room," she says.

What was my first thought? Is my mother here? Then I experience a pang of remorse since I haven't thought about my mother in a long time. I did have a nice dream about her recently, but I'm keeping it to myself until my next session with my therapist.

"Oh?" I ask. "My mom?"

"Yes. "I think I feel your father as well," she says. "But he is nowhere near as strong as the female presence."

"What does she want?" I inquire. "Is she saying anything?"

"She wants you to know it's all okay."

"OK," I say, but I'm wondering — but not asking — why don't you see Ed? Why is he not here?

I definitely feel better after the session. The discomfort isn't completely gone, but it's less acute, and my neck has more mobility. I scheduled another appointment. Actually, I made one more for this week and two for the week after that. I felt dizzy and light-headed on the way home, despite the fact that she never came near to breaking my neck, which would release a vertiginous stream of toxins, as other chiropractors have done in the past.

I'm still thinking about the session hours later. I appreciated the woo-woo, but I'm curious what it means that my mother was present. What did she mean when she said, "It's all okay?" Is she still with me? Is she always by my side? I believe there is more to life than we can see. I'm aware that some folks see more than others. When I look in the mirror, I notice aspects about myself that others don't notice. They see things I don't see when they look at me. The fact that something is not visible to everyone does not imply that it is not genuine.

I do see Ed after I go to bed. My chamber is dark, and I think to myself, Oh, there you are. I understand how that sounds. But this isn't the first time he's come to see me. A few days after he died, I was laying in bed, half awake and almost asleep, when I sensed a presence in the room and knew it was him. I shouted out, "I love you." I'm missing you. "I hope you understand how much you were loved."

It would have been a lot easier to convince myself that I was making everything up, but I certainly saw him. I also heard him. He looked at me and murmured, "Oh," in the sweet, empathetic way that he had for reacting to sensitive situations. Then I felt pressure on the centre of my forehead, as if he was pressing his finger against it. He had really distinct hands, exquisite hands, and I was sure he was telling me through this gesture that he was fine and that I shouldn't be sad— at least not too sad. Everything will be OK. The more I've moved away from that October night, the more I've wondered, Did it actually happen? I even offered a challenge one day. "Okay, Ed, if I ever see a green cat, you have to come visit me and tell me everything is fine," I remarked at the beach. However, after my mother arrived earlier today and assured me the same thing—it'll be fine—I've decided to stop asking. Everything must be fine.

They are, in fact. By the following week, the heaviness and anxiety that had made me immobile have gradually lifted, allowing me to get back on track, beginning with the most basic of remedies—movement. I take a vigorous walk in the neighbourhood with Luna every morning after my coffee. I take in the fresh air and relish the prospect of a new day. Birds are chirping. The leaves are glistening with dew. As the sun breaks through the clouds, it warms. The air is alive with hope and possibilities. It's similar to a joyful medicine. Why don't I do this more frequently?

My heart is pounding. My knees hurt, and my neck and back are reluctant partners, but they're getting better. I fight the impulse to step on the scale. What is it going to say to me if I can't feel it?

I treat myself to a nice smoothie at home. I combine bananas, almond butter, almond milk, rolled oats, honey, and the half-cup of coffee that, more than anything else, keeps me going. I pour it into a lovely glass and garnish with a few sprigs of mint from my garden. Why not reward myself with a good presentation? More importantly, why not treat myself nicely?

It does make a difference. When I sit down at my desk, I am not only excited to get to work, but I am also filled with thankfulness. I was so caught up in my woe-is-me that I missed this crucial aspect. Valerie's Home Cooking is about home cooking at a time when everyone in the world is cooking at home and longing for the comfort of great, uncomplicated meals. I can almost hear Norman Lear encouraging me, when I was fifteen, to "go get 'em, kid." Except it's my mother, grandmother, and great-grandmother who give me the thumbs up.

It truly is a fresh season in so many ways—for the show, for myself, for everyone. Life is a vast table where we're expected to feed and nourish each other. "Pull up a chair," Ruth Reichl, the renowned culinary writer, once said. "Try a bite."

I'm getting ideas. A fresh Bolognese sauce for an easier lasagna. Sliders with ham, apple, and cheddar. A jar of marinara sauce on my kitchen counter suggests a fairly classic baked ziti with a mix of chopped vegetables in my slow cooker. I dig through my mother's recipe box for the well-worn card for her onion rings. I make them—and then leave them in the oven for far too long. Wolfie refers to them as overdonion rings.

"But they're delicious," he points out.

My first production meeting is on Zoom with Mary Beth Bray, who is now an executive producer, and culinary producer Sophie Clark, and I am excited to discuss my ideas. My favourite part of the show is selecting the meals for each episode. But first, we have a lot of catching up to do before we dive into the recipes and divide them into discrete episodes. We haven't seen each other since March 2020, when we cut the previous season short by three episodes and said our final goodbyes due to the shutdown.

"How's everyone doing?" I inquire. "It's wonderful to see your smiling faces. "I've been missing you."

During the hiatus, Mary Beth relocated from New York to Los Angeles with her family. She gives some specifics on their cross-country trip, the majority of which include small restaurants they stopped at and her delicious discoveries along the way. Sophie and I are taking notes.

The episodes are swiftly put together. Lemony cacio e pepe and homemade pretzel buns with butter and ham are among the recipes, as are salmon sliders and buffalo chicken burgers, as well as a spring roll salad with peanut butter dressing and a quinoa, sweet potato, and black bean bowl with cilantro yoghourt dressing. Orange vanilla bean angel food cake, no-bake chocolate peanut butter bars, no-churn lemon ice cream, and almond butter, oat, and cranberry cookies are among the desserts.

Even though the shows are meant to be timeless, I'd like to address Covid and speak directly to viewers about spending more time in the kitchen this year, and everyone thinks that this makes sense. So we invited my friend, food writer Jo Stougaard, to be my first episode guest. Her nephew works as a firefighter, and his wife works as a nurse. I'll pack a picnic basket for Jo to bring to them. Smoked turkey sandwiches with Calabrian chilli aioli, homemade salt and vinegar potato chips, and no-campfire s'mores.

The episode is shot in a house with a newly renovated kitchen. I'm giddy with joy and excitement because I'm back on set. Almost everyone involved in the production has been with the show from its inception. We assemble in the backyard before we begin. Everyone is veiled; everyone has been tested. I appreciate everyone's input. It would be impossible to put on the show differently. Mary Beth expresses those sentiments, thanking God for the good health we've all had.

"It's a new season," she announces. "Let's have some fun."

By April, all of the episodes would have been shot and edited. A thirteenth season of the show has also been ordered. I'm sure I won't be as tormented next time. In addition to continuing my morning walks and creating new smoothie flavours, I've added an afternoon workout—25 to 45 minutes on my Peloton bike. In a departure from the past, the training did not begin as a punishment for being overweight, even if I am not satisfied with my current weight. The distinction is that I do not despise myself. I was feeling terrific and wanted to feel even better. My body truly desired the workout, and I was delighted to oblige.

It's been six months since Ed died, and I'm learning every day that sadness doesn't go away so much as it morphs into something manageable. I'll still cry when Wolfie has a question or an issue and my first reaction is, "Let's call your dad"—which, of course, we can't. Other times, I am surrounded by wonderful memories that I wear like jewellery, knowing that they make me sparkle. Then there are the days when I forget and carry on with my life until I come upon a reminder.

That is exactly what occurred last night.

I climbed into bed and began browsing through TikTok, like I often do. Something on the screen caught my eye just as I was about to place my phone on my nightstand. It was only a small green dump truck. Three kittens lived inside the truck. I recalled the challenge I'd offered to Ed a few months before. You must return to me if I see a green cat. Cats in a green toy dump truck counted? I was too tired to laugh, but I thought to myself, How ridiculous, and turned off my phone before pulling up the blankets, settling into my pillows, and closing my eyes.

I'm not sure how much time had passed, whether seconds, minutes, or hours, but I was drifting in that half-asleep, half-awake state when I became aware of a presence in the room. Ed appeared in the darkness when I opened my eyes. Take a look at me. He has that Cheshire cat grin. As if you asked for it. I'm here.

"What's going on?" I inquired. "Are you sure you're really here?"

Ed remained silent. But then, whoosh, I felt like I was being taken up through the roof into the night sky, where I saw the stars glittering and sparkling into infinity, a celestial light show that was gorgeous, bright, exhilarating, and infinite. It was as if I were being questioned, "Do you want to feel joy?" What are your thoughts on this?

Then I found myself back in bed, either still sleepy or fully sleeping, I'm not sure. But I was exceedingly peaceful, warm, at ease, and intrigued.

"Is this your name?" "Are you present?" I inquired once more.

There was no response.

"All right, if you're here, play it for me." Only you will understand what I mean. So do it for me."

There was a flash of light in the corner of the room, near the ceiling. When I turned my head, I noticed a small screen. It was immediately followed by the sound of a guitar. I was half expecting to see Patrick Swayze hovering over Demi Moore at the potter's wheel by this point. But all I heard was the sound of Ed's guitar playing a mix of the intro to "Women in Love..." and Wolfie's song "Think It Over." It was a completely unique mash-up done just by Ed, a little something I liked blended with something he liked, and I knew he was making it specifically for me.

When he was done, the small light went off, and he took me up and floated me around the room one more time before placing me in the bed. I didn't need any more proof at this point. There are some things you can't explain and don't want or need to explain, and this was one of them. I leaned forward to kiss him and felt the pressure of someone grabbing me as well as the stubble on his face.

"I love you," I whispered as I drifted off to sleep.

I never heard his voice, but I awoke with the distinct impression that not only were things fine, but that excellent things were on their way.

Listen, I get how insane this sounds. I do. And perhaps it was all a dream. But it felt genuine to me, and whatever gets us through these difficult times. You know what I mean?

Now for the real kicker. I sent word to Ed after spending the remainder of the day pondering about what happened and wondering how I could know all those facts if it didn't really happen, as well as feeling pretty happy about everything. Last night was incredible and special, and I would want to see you again, but not tonight. I'm sixty-one years old and exhausted. I can't spend every night floating around the stars.

CHAPTER 15

THE LITTLE GIRL NEEDS A HUG

APRIL 2021

STop everything. I have got breaking news. I think there is a very good chance that I am an innately happy, joyful person who just needed sixty-one years to recognize it. Gawd, I am thinking what a doofus I have been. Time is too precious to have wasted so much of it. Let me try to explain what finally happened.

1. Don't laugh, but it starts with cat videos

I watch cat videos on TikTok almost every morning before I get out of bed. This is not an uncommon practice. It is a genuine phenomenon with billions of views. Over the years, experts have shown that watching cat videos can actually help individuals relax and de-stress. According to Wikipedia, "feelings of guilt when postponing tasks can be reduced by watching cat videos."

In other words, viewing cat videos makes procrastinators feel better about themselves. The reason we procrastinate is left unspoken. We're doing it because we're watching cat videos. I think that as long as the home isn't on fire, our affection for cats takes precedence over almost everything.

I wandered into other areas of TikTok one day because of my love of viewing cat videos. I came across the deja vu challenge, where TikTok users post videos of themselves lip-syncing to Olivia Rodrigo's song "Deja Vu" while using the app's inverted filter to toggle back and forth between their mirror image and an inverted image of themselves. This inverted image appears to depict how others perceive you.

This is usually done by girls and young women, and many of them are said to have difficulty seeing the inverted image of themselves. In theory, this is due to the fact that we never see and remain unaware of our true selves. We usually only see ourselves in images or in a mirror. A mirror shows us a mirror picture of ourselves and merely verifies what we are used to telling ourselves about what we see or want to see.

The inverted filter, on the other hand, displays a different view, the one that others see when they look at us. It purportedly removes our personal biases toward ourselves and presents who we truly are.

I'm interested.

I obviously have problems.

I've been dealing with this problem since I appeared on the Today show over a year and a half ago and basically said, "Enough !". "How do I move on with my life and find joy in the body I have now?" That doesn't mean I'm happy with how I look. Yes, I need to shed some weight. I may have to reduce my food intake, forgo an extra glass of wine, and ride my bike an extra day or two every week. I'd like to be healthy. But I no longer want to torture myself. I can't be as imperfect as I continuously tell myself I am at this age, at least not to the extent that it precludes me from enjoying everything else.

And, of course, everyone says I'm correct, that I'm smart, funny, and gorgeous. Or they just state, "You're insane."

And Angie Johnsey has provided me with methods to deal with the voice in my head that always says, "you need to lose ten pounds and then..."

And I feel like I'm getting somewhere.

However, for some reason, I continue to give more attention to individuals who insult me on the Internet rather than those who admire the images and videos I share. Why do I believe the naysayers? Why am I not believing in lovely people?

I understand why. Old habits die slowly. The negative comments are more credible. They confirm the terrible things I've been telling myself. How can I believe those who say I'm attractive when I don't see it myself?

Which is why I'm intrigued by, and perhaps a little terrified by, this inverted filter. What do other people think of me? How will I react to seeing myself in this light?

I have no idea what I'll see when I take out my phone, log into TikTok, and record a video of myself using the inverted filter. Will I cry like other people do when they see themselves? ("OMG, I'm in tears!") Is that how people see me?") Will I witness proof of all the haters have observed and stated over the years? I'm not wearing any makeup and my hair is pulled back. I look like this after a workout when I'm flushed, sweaty, plain, and, in my opinion, at my ugliest.

The video lasts less than a minute. I gasp as I see it for the first time. "Oh, my God, I'm my mom!" I scream.

I catch a glimpse of her and shudder with the jolt of recognition.

Then I rewatch it. And then some. After the third time, I press pause and stare at the screen, where I see myself, not my mother, and for the first time in my life, I realise I'm not unattractive.

It is revolutionary. I'm not unattractive.

I'm in tears. I'm not unattractive.

It may appear strange that a short video on a gimmicky app can have this effect, but it can. It liberates something within me. I feel as though I stepped outside for the first time in a long time and saw sunlight. And I see myself in that quick flicker. For the first time in my life, I can see what other people see when they look at me...

2. I am going to skip that part for a moment

Life becomes so hectic that I can feel normal sneaking into the picture. The week before my birthday, I got my second Covid immunisation. There is no reaction, but I take it easy. Wolfie spent the weekend signing thousands of copies of his upcoming album, which will be released in June, and Patrick and I put them back in the enormous brown boxes they came in. It's like if we're running a small family business. I had to prepare for a cooking demonstration for the USO. Then I met with my producer and culinary producer to start planning Valerie's Home Cooking season thirteen.

Wolfie arrives with a box of SusieCakes cupcakes for my birthday. The box also includes two slices of their lemon cake, which is my favourite. I want to remember this photo of me celebrating my 61st birthday. My smile is more genuine than the one that millions of people witnessed when I was in a swimsuit more than a decade ago. The headline on the cover of People magazine shouted, BIKINI BOD AT 48!, as if the editors couldn't believe I'd shed more than forty pounds and was in the best shape of my life.

However, appearances can be deceiving. I had to almost starve myself for a week before the photo shoot in order to feel comfortable in a bikini, and I clearly didn't lose the weight. Take a look at me. As soon as the shot was over, I began to regain it. Would I ever go that far again? No way. I figured out something else, something different and, in the long run, healthier for me. I'm sorry for the message I sent to folks back then. I contributed to the problem of diet culture and making women feel bad about themselves unless they reached a certain number on the scale.

Hey, I wasn't immune either. Even though I was dieting and exercising like an Olympic athlete, I was made to feel horrible if I had a little pouch on the side or weighed a little over than my target weight that week. The entire experience opened my eyes to truths I had never considered before. Like how many folks in the health-diet-beauty businesses capitalise on our inadequacies. Like how the apparel industry's sizing irregularities make us feel bad. It's as though they're always shifting the goalposts. Marilyn Monroe was a size sixteen in her day. Today, she will be six. What's the story? She weighed 156 pounds and stood 5'6". I can't think of a more lovely lady. She was all natural and curvaceous.

While I'm on a tirade, why do we use the term "plus-size model"? Why don't we have a term like "super tiny and skinny model" if we do that? Why do we have to categorise and judge? These words have been distorted and weaponized: full-size, mid-size, husky. Sizes should be global, guilt-free, and established and maintained with one goal in mind: to assist individuals in selecting apparel that fits their body and makes them feel good about it.

I'm obviously enthusiastic about this. I'm not sure how to express how I feel about all of this and my role in it other than to apologise and explain that I was under the same influence as everyone else. I broadcast the message that I would only feel happy if I shed x number of pounds and went into a bikini. I, too, believed it. The big reveal not only put pressure on me, but it also caused others to look critically at their own bodies and think of themselves as not bikini ready, while the truth is that there is no such thing as a beach body or bikini ready. There is no such thing, I repeat. And I apologise if I mislead anyone to assume there was. When it comes to being beach and swimsuit ready, I have a friend whose daughter is a therapist who works with women and girls who have body and food issues, and she gives them a simple and clear message: "Get dressed—and if you're okay with the level of camel toe, there's no nip slip, and you don't have food in your teeth, you're good to go."

I have a more straightforward message. Do whatever makes you happy about yourself. Do not try to be anything other than who you are. You can exercise. You are capable of losing weight. God knows I strive to do both, and lately I've been succeeding more than not. However, do not confuse this with dieting. I take care of myself in a way that fits my lifestyle and mental health, which involves treating the pain and unhappiness I see in the mirror rather than the weight, knowing that if I do, I will naturally arrive at the optimal weight for me.

3. Two weeks after my second vaccination, I meet my girlfriends for a belated birthday dinner at Casa Vega, our favourite neighbourhood Mexican restaurant

It's the first time any of us have gotten together in over a year. We sit outside for several hours, eating, talking, and toasting each other with margaritas. Being together in person, laughing and exchanging smiles, is like oxygen being pumped into my lungs. We stand in the parking lot at the end of the night and hold each other, not wanting to let the night or each other go.

I was missing you.

I adore you.

It's hard to realise it's been over a year.

I adore you.

I adore you.

We're all in our sixties. We sound like a group of fifth-grade ladies who went out to supper without our parents and had the time of our lives.

I'm still glowing as I get ready for bed at home. I wash my face and change into my pyjamas. I intend to read for a while, but when I reach for the book on my nightstand, my hand is drawn to my phone instead. I know you shouldn't keep your phone so close to your bed.

In any case, I do. It's the adolescent in me. Something might happen, and I'll need to know right away. I'll have to capture a picture of the kitties lying out across the bed in the morning. The only thing I won't use it for is making or receiving phone calls. Hey, we're all different.

My plan is to watch a few TikTok cat videos. But then I watched my own TikTok video. I'm curious if I'll have the same reaction as I did two weeks ago. It's even better this time. I'm not only looking for someone who isn't ugly. I notice someone I like. I see eyes that are filled with compassion. I recognize my fragility. I see someone who has made an effort to be a decent daughter and sister. I see someone who did an excellent job as a mother. I see someone who is dedicated to their work. I notice someone with a good sense of humour. I see someone who can laugh and laugh loudly. I see someone who is willing to participate. I notice someone who is concerned. I see someone who hasn't always given her all, but has tried and continues to try. I see someone who aspires to be a grandmother. I also see a female that needs to drop some weight. At the same time, I notice someone who is finally coming to life.

I believe I see what others may see, strangers who always say they can relate to me; I believe I see the type of person who doesn't have to pretend to have it all together, who is a real human being, not perfect and not even attempting to be great, just trying to be nice. I can see the goodness in my eyes. I also see someone attempting to be her true self. There is no makeup on. The hair was pulled back. Clear vision. She's also beaming. She's a little girl—the little girl who has always sought to amuse and make people happy. Only now are the voices telling her not to. She's simply being herself. I can tell she wants to be hugged. She requires a hug. I offer her a hug, knowing that if I keep touching her, she will get stronger. She only requires love. Everything comes down to love.I delete the movie, turn out the light, and go to bed. I'm going to get some rest.

4. I guest on The Secret Life of Cookies podcast

During the podcast, the host, Marissa Rothkopf, a brilliant culinary writer, complimented me on being a happy person and questions how and why that is, and if I have always been that way. Instead of my usual glib retort, "Well, you just choose happy," I offer a bit of what this past year has been like and how I have worked to clear up the pigpen of messages that has resided in my head for much of my life (imagine Charlie Brown's pal), and in doing so, I come to realise that (a) I like this voice, I really like this voice that is in my head and coming out of my mouth, and (b) joy and happiness

Others have always seen it, and now, with the work I've been doing since meeting Angie, plus everything else that has pushed me to take a long, hard, and honest look at how I view myself today, at this age, in this body, I'm ready to embrace myself as joyous and happy. I'm ready to own it and chase it, knowing that some days will be more difficult than others, but that it's always within my grasp. It is always within me. It has always existed. It is the default option for me. But I can hear it now.

I sat down with a glass of great chardonnay a little later and thought to myself, Huh, you know what? I am content.

I realise that sounds strange.

It's also strange.

It also feels fantastic.

CHAPTER 16

THE HOUSE I WANT TO DIE IN

MAY 2021

Hello and welcome to my seaside cottage. The four-bedroom Cape Cod-style mansion lies atop a cliff, but you'd never guess it from the street. Pass through the entrance between the garage and the guest house, however, and you'll be met with a sight that will take your breath away. It happens every time, no matter how many times people come here, including me—and I bought the house in 1984, when I was twenty-four, had few costs, and could afford it after a decade on a top-rated TV show.

A lengthy, slanted staircase descends to the seashore. It's a genuine wow from wherever you stand, especially when dolphins and whales swim nearby, which happens frequently. It's as though they recognize us and stop by to say, "Hey, what's up?" You can hear the waves even with your eyes closed, and when the swells get enormous and break hard, the ground shakes, and you can't help but stop and scream, "Wow!"

I drove here yesterday and met Wolfie, Andraia, Patrick, and Stacy, who have all been staying here for quite some time. I'm not sure how long they've been here, and they've lost track of time, which occurs at the beach. Patrick is correct when he claims it's impossible to be productive here. Your mind goes on vacation, and your body moves in slow motion. Everything takes an extra thirty minutes. With the exception of cocktail hour. That seems to be becoming earlier and sooner.

But I have more than just chilling on my itinerary. Despite its beautiful setting, the house is in serious need of repair. Pipes leak, some rooms have water damage and mildew, and there are serious structural difficulties, on top of corrosion from sun, wind, fog, and sea water exposure, as well as age-related issues. The house, in its current form, reminds me of a senior citizen who, after suffering through one of those dreadful, convulsive coughing fits, realises she made a tactical mistake by spending decades without seeing her doctor.

It is my fault for the neglect. I let the problems pile up until they took over, just like everything else in my life. That is finally about to change. Years of work and discussions with my architect have resulted in a concrete blueprint. The present house will be demolished at the end of the summer, and a new house will be built in its place. It took me three years to come to terms with the design. My phone is filled with images of my architect's renderings. That is why I have driven to the shore. I'm all set to show Wolfie and my brother.

It's usual for me to take this long. In fact, given how quickly I generally go, this timetable is extremely brisk. It also perfectly reflects what I've been going through and where I aim to be in the future. I was looking for something in the kitchen around five years ago. I opened many drawers and was immediately overwhelmed by the amount of debris. When I went through the cabinets, the same thing happened. Too much stuff was stuffed into every possible space—things I didn't need or want. I eventually gave up my quest and realised I needed to renovate the kitchen—and possibly a few other rooms.

I met with my architect, who had previously renovated my house in the hills, so he was familiar with me and understood what he was getting into. I was open and honest as I showed him around, saying that the house had a slew of issues that I had let accumulate over the years. I could have been talking to my therapist as I discussed what worked and what didn't, what I liked and disliked about the house, and what I wanted to alter. It was my entire existence.

"I've let some things go," I said.

"Everyone else does." He laughed.

"I was pregnant with Wolfie the last time I redid anything around here."

"How much older is he now?"

"Almost thirty."

"Wow, then it's finally time." He smiled once more.

"I love this house," I declared. "I don't even know how much needs to be changed."

"How much of your life do you want to change?" he inquired.

"We can knock down some barriers." However, I do not wish to alter the footprint."

"Okay. The imprint remains. It is effective for you."

"Yes."

"What is it that doesn't work for you?"

Thank god he already knew how difficult any kind of change was for me. But this mansion was in a class by itself. I was passionately attached to it and determined to preserve its history. There had been so much happening in it. I fell in love with it the moment I saw it. The house was deserted. It had been rebuilt after a recent wildfire swept down the hills, leapt the Pacific Coast Highway, and destroyed it and the other homes. But I could see it was in shock. I pledged to look after it and provide it with rich and happy lives. My parents initially lived there full-time. My brothers and their wives would come and go. Ed and I spent the weekends and holidays there. I had a miscarriage in the upper bedroom in 1985. My father and Ed had their famed fistfight there a few years later. Dad and Patrick repainted the exterior several times. Even when I altered the original blue colour to yellow, I kept calling it the "blue house." We had fantastic Super Bowl parties there, played volleyball, and ran around on the beach.

I surprised Ed with a surprise 30th birthday party in this house, but we arrived four hours late because I couldn't get him out of the studio. "Why do I have to go all the way out to the beach to celebrate my birthday?" he wondered. I wanted to slam him. I can still hear myself making a call to the house. "We haven't even left yet."

"But you already said that two hours ago."

"Tell that to the birthday boy."

Before Van Halen headed to Cabo, MTV shot here. Sammy Hagar purchased a home two doors up. It was a terrific spot to hang out and unwind, which Ed excelled at. Patrick would marvel at Ed's ability to lounge on the couch watching TV with a guitar on his lap and play "the most insane stuff without even seeming to think about what he was doing." "He wasn't even listening," my brother would say. "And yet you could see him staring off into the distance, pulling these ideas in from some other planet."

After Wolfie started kindergarten and I got to know some of the other moms, this became the perfect site for us to meet on a Friday afternoon and sit on the bluff with a glass of wine and watch the sunset while our kids played in the yard. Ed maintained the Coldwater Canyon house with the studio and I got the beach house when we divorced, but I still let him use it whenever he wanted. When I walked out the next day after he had left, I discovered that he had neglected to turn off the stove burner. He was in a bad mood. He could have destroyed the house, as well as the entire neighbourhood. On January 1, 2011, I married Tom on the terrace. Ed was there that night, as were my parents, brothers, and closest friends. Everyone in my life has been there and contributed to the creation of memories, and I can still see and hear them when I look around. I can go there and sit on the bluff and feel my parents' presence. Ed is available for discussion. Wolfie is racing around with his mates. Everyone remains present. That is what has most concerned me about this remodelling job. I can be alone there and still be around the people I care about. I'm alright with meeting new people and making new memories, but I don't want to forget the past. I can't seem to let go.

"That's always the problem," my architect pointed out. "What do you save?" What do you alter? "What exactly do you get rid of?"

We were sitting at the dining table, and he was prepared to reveal his new intentions to me for the first time. He pushed his iPad toward me, explaining that he had made three-dimensional animations of the new house that would allow me to see the street view outside as well as the various rooms within, including views of the ocean from several balconies. I took a deep breath and started scrolling, nervous. I began to cry a few moments later. That was not what either of us expected. I believe I went into shock.

"It's not my house," I pointed out. "It's not the blue house."

It's not even close. It appeared from the front to be the exterior of a covered bridge in the Vermont countryside. The back was open, modern, and barnlike, a wood and glass salute to family and the outdoors. Inside, it was all about light, space, and views of the ocean, with plenty of places to gather, including a ground-level patio that seemed to flow out of the kitchen and reminded me of alfresco dining in Italy via Malibu.

When I finished looking at the photos, my tears had been replaced with awe, and I was dumbfounded. It was one of those rare occasions when the future revealed itself, and while I wasn't ready to make any firm decisions, I loved what I saw. I was not only impressed, but also excited—and terrified. My architect had studied me, listened to me, and returned with his interpretation of my journey from the time I bought the house until now. He painted a vision of transformation, progress, and possibilities for me.

He actually demonstrated my potential.

"I think I like it," I said. "It frightens me. In a positive manner, of course. But I'd want to think about it for a while."

Three years turned out to be a long time. I am now prepared to present Wolfie and my brother. It's a Sunday afternoon, and the sun is shining brightly, transforming the water into a dazzling show of diamonds. Wolfie is wrapping up an interview with a radio station, while Patrick and Stacy are preparing to return to their Arizona home. I was barefoot in the kitchen, preparing grilled jalapeno peppers packed with ground turkey and cheese for a late lunch. Someone requests spicy sauce. Another person desires water. I'm laughing. I'm a cook, a waitress, a mother, a sister, and just Valerie— exactly as I like it, especially here at the beach house.

Then it's time to go. I gather everyone at the table, remind them of the path that led to the images they are about to view, and then hand them my phone. Wolfie and Patrick are initially calm. They move through the animations without saying anything. Then they can't stop exclaiming one superlative after another. Oh my goodness. Amazing. I still can't believe it. Incredible.

Wolfie wraps his arms around me and squeezes.

"It's so cool, Mom," he exclaims.

"I know," I admit. "It's... it's... it's big."

It's hardly the only significant change. There's the Tom situation. We've split up. Fissures in the relationship occurred years earlier, and the lockdown resulted in a severe rethinking of priorities, as it did for nearly everyone I know. What do I desire versus what do I require? What is assisting me in moving forward in my life? What is it that is holding me back? I started asking those questions before Covid, and I still do. In order to feel more joy, I must identify and let go of concepts and behaviours that no longer serve me, and one of these is my eleven-year marriage to Tom.

The decision was slow and hard. But we've strayed from the interests that brought us together and discovered that those differences can't be mended. He is a good man who is dealing with many of the same challenges that I am: What can he do to give his life meaning and purpose? Where can he find happiness? What does he care about? What has he discovered? And what will he do differently in the future?

The routes we believed we were taking shifted. It does not imply that we are evil people. That we are human. I only want the best for him. As for me, I understand that separating could mean spending the rest of my life alone, and if that is the case, I am willing to try and will approach it without fear or regret. As many women will point out, being single does not imply being available. It also does not imply being unavailable. It can refer to bcing autonomous, confident, content, adventurous, searching, inquiring, or working on something.

That is all true, and I am eager to see what occurs next.

I don't want to waste any more time. This past year has taught me and everyone else the value of time. I gave up hunting for a magical number. I turned sixty years old. My second marriage is coming to an end. My first husband, my soulmate, passed away. I faced grief, both mine and my son's. I returned to work. I was immunised. And I wondered, "What have I learned from this?" How have I evolved? What will I strive to do differently in the future?

Many of us are feeling the same way and trying to figure out how to emerge stronger and wiser. I believe we got a good look at some significant issues that have gone unnoticed for far too long, and we realise it's time to address them—and ourselves. I believe we all understand that we are supposed to be better and kinder to one another.

Wolfie adds another memorable memory to the beach home later that afternoon, as we sit talking and listening to the waves, when he informs me that he started writing his record here at the beach. I had absolutely no notion. He moved out of his flat and into the guest home here after finishing the Van Halen tour in 2012.

"I didn't want to live with either of you or with Dad," he explains.

Moored in the middle of nothing, he taught himself Logic Pro and wrote "Mammoth."

He asks if I would like to hear the demo.

"Uh, yes," I answered emphatically. "Duh, of course I want to hear it."

Wolfie tries to play it through the living room speakers, but it doesn't work. He also can't get it to play on the smaller kitchen speakers. His annoyance is shown in a juvenile growl: "The Internet here is messed up." He eventually plays it on his **phone**, and the original is quite similar to the final version—a beautiful, powerful, and even happy song about living with despair.

"I love those lyrics," I say. It is not acceptable to stand up and walk away... everything is conceivable.

"Thanks, Ma," he says.

"That's my boy," I explained.

I give myself a second or two before correcting myself. I gaze out the window at the crisscrossing clouds in the sky and whisper quietly, Hey, that's our boy.

Then I get up and say I'm going for a **stroll** before supper. I make my way to the beach through the stairwell. It's a total of 104 steps down to the beach, followed by 104 steps **back** up. But guess what? It's time to stop counting steps and just enjoy the freakin' walk.

You understand what I mean?

The contents of this book may not be copied, reproduced or transmitted without the express written permission of the author or publisher. Under no circumstances will the publisher or author be responsible or liable for any damages, compensation or monetary loss arising from the information contained in this book, whether directly or indirectly. .

Disclaimer Notice:

Although the author and publisher have made every effort to ensure the accuracy and completeness of the content, they do not, however, make any representations or warranties as to the accuracy, completeness, or reliability of the content. , suitability or availability of the information, products, services or related graphics contained in the book for any purpose. Readers are solely responsible for their use of the information contained in this book

Every effort has been made to make this book possible. If any omission or error has occurred unintentionally, the author and publisher will be happy to acknowledge it in upcoming versions.

Made in United States
Troutdale, OR
12/08/2023